Finding Our Way
TOGETHER

Bible Study Handbook
Book 4

For leaders of house groups

INTERNATIONAL BIBLE READING ASSOCIATION

Cover photograph: Twenty-five Educational
Editor: Joy Mead
Illustrations (pages 32, 35, 39, 41, 44, 46, 49 and 51): Tansy Patilla
Illustrations (pages 70, 73, 75, 77 and 79): Bill Denning

Published by:
The International Bible Reading Association
1020 Bristol Road
Selly Oak
Birmingham
Great Britain
B29 6LB

ISBN 0–7197–0974–1
ISSN 140–8593

Typeset by Christian Education Publications

CONTENTS

These themes match those in *Words For Today 2001* and *Light For Our Path 2001*, so that they can be used by groups who use IBRA's daily Bible readings, but they are also designed to be used by any group at any time.

THE WRITERS

Edmund Banyard – a minister and former Moderator of the General Assembly of the United Reformed Church.

Tina Beattie – a Roman Catholic working as a freelance lecturer and writer in theology. She has a special interest in issues relating to women in the church, and in the symbolism and theology of the Virgin Mary.

Anna Briggs – an artist and writer, living near Cambridge, a member of the Iona Community and a team member of a Local Ecumenical Project along with her husband. She has worked all her life in community work, often unpaid, and struggles with the impact of loss and a brain injury on her life. She is happiest working in paint, fabric, thread and colour, sharing the enjoyment of creation with people she meets.

Graeme Brown – a minister of the Church of Scotland and a member of the Iona Community.

Judith Chapman – a minister in the Clay Cross Circuit of the Methodist Church.

Stephen Dawes – a minister and Chair of the Cornwall District of the Methodist Church

Bill Denning – a Methodist minister who runs retreats and workshops exploring the close links between creativity and spirituality.

Joy Mead – a poet, freelance writer and editor.

Jean Mortimer – a minister in the United Reformed Church for 32 years; taught New Testament Greek in the University of Leeds; now involved in theological education through the Scottish Churches Open College in Edinburgh.

Val Ogden – a former member of the NCEC staff, who served with the United Church of Zambia and is now a minister in the Wolverhampton Methodist Circuit.

Jayne Scott – Principal of the Scottish Churches Open College, an ecumenical theological college which offers part-time distance learning opportunities for anyone who is interested. Trained as a Baptist minister and committed to the task of theological education as a process of community transformation, Jane enjoys working closely with groups who are not afraid to ask questions, especially in relation to justice and peace issues.

Acknowledgements

The editor and publisher express thanks for permission to use copyright items. Every effort has been made to trace copyright owners, but if any rights have been inadvertently overlooked, the necessary amendments will be made in subsequent editions.

Useful addresses

Amnesty International (British Section): 99–119 Rosebery Avenue, London EC1R 4RE.

Catholic Fund for Overseas Development (CAFOD): 2 Romero Close, Stockwell Road, London SW9 9TY.

Christian Aid, One World Week and **Churches Together in Britain and Ireland (CTBI)**: Inter-Church House, 35–41 Lower Marsh, London SE1 7RL.

Oxfam: 274 Banbury Road, Oxford OX2 2DZ.

World Council of Churches: 150 Route de Ferney, 1211 Geneva 2, Switzerland.

World Federation of the United Nations Association (UNA): Pavillon du Petit Caconnex, 16 Avenue Jean Trembley, Geneva, Switzerland.

What is the group for?

Before you begin using this book, think carefully about your group's reason for being. Why have people gathered together? It might help to remember the title of this book: *Finding Our Way Together* – the process is our concern. What will matter is the way the group works and dreams together those dreams that cannot be dreamed alone. Dreams and visions, hopes and longings are often about sharing.

A group exists to share, explore, enable and empower. Its focus should be to enhance the diversity of its members as well as to explore images and symbols shared and re-discover lost visions and dreams. A good group will endeavour to do justice to the variety and richness of its members and the community to which they belong. How it does this will differ according to the regional, cultural and spiritual inheritance of its members. Everyone comes to a group with a lot of baggage. Shedding some of it will be part of the experience of growing together.

Important aspects of the gathering together will be creative listening to what is said and what is not said, and the sharing of experiences in response to stories, images and poems. Finding our way means making our own path, exploring thoughts, feelings, ideas, experiences. Sharing feelings openly and consciously is a high level of communication – probably the highest – and will often be about questions ... and more questions. It is unlikely to be about expressing a pre-rehearsed set of theories or opinions ... or about finding easy and comforting answers.

No one person should monopolize conversation. Theological 'soap-boxes' should be avoided. Remember this is about discovery – finding the way, together. The way is not mapped out or laid down – you have to make it. As you do so, remember that if you stay on the road you are on you will surely get where you are going. Keep checking that you are on the road you want to be on!

The group has a shared responsibility to make sure each person is included and valued, but a good enabler is of immense value.

A good enabler will:

- prepare well, remembering what seems obvious: that what is best for the group will depend upon who is coming;
- look at the *Preparation* section and make sure that all that is required is available;
- remember that direct eye contact is important in a small group, and arrange seating sensitively and perceptively with this in mind;
- be punctual and not allow the meeting to drag on;
- read and understand the Bible passages, be ready for questions, and make sure everyone understands fully and is following;
- be prepared to introduce different images and writings to encourage responses so that many facets of the theme appear;
- have the *Aim* clearly in mind throughout and go back to it at the end, to see if it has been achieved;
- help people to feel at ease;
- maintain eye contact when telling stories;
- be sensitive to the feelings and expectations of others;
- respect confidences;
- challenge the group to act;
- try different methods with enthusiasm;
- have a sense of humour;
- care for the group and encourage openness and honesty;
- avoid extremes;
- explore what our Christian understanding says to us about relationships with people of other faiths and those who maintain they have no faith;
- make sure the group works harmoniously, looking for signs of discomfort or boredom and responding to them.

Above all, remember what Jesus said the last time he was with his special small group of friends:

'I give you a new commandment: love one another; as I have loved you, so you are to love one another. If there is this love among you, then everyone will know that you are my disciples.'

(John 13.34–35, REB)

Other books in this series

Book 1 comprises shorter themes, including:
   Jesus – Man of mystery *(3 sessions)*
   God's *shalom (3 sessions)*
   The Kingdom is for children *(2 sessions)*
   The power of prayer *(2 sessions)*

Book 2 includes:
   God's world – God's Mission *(7 sessions)*
   The Jesus we meet *(6 sessions)*
   Parables for our time *(3 sessions)*
   Pilgrimage *(4 sessions)*

Book 3 includes:
   Readings from the Gospel of John *(6 weeks)*
   Living encounters – with people of other faiths *(4 weeks)*
   Building community *(10 weeks)*
   Voices of creation *(5 weeks)*

GOSPEL STORIES FOR TODAY

Study 1 'Let me tell you a story ...'

AIM

Keynote readings
Matthew 2.1–12
Luke 7.36–50

To bring and accept the mysterious, growing gift of stories.

PREPARATION

Ask members of the group to think about the story of the three wise men and bring with them to the meeting their own re-telling of the story for today or other versions they like.

'What shall I bring...'
Read together Matthew 2.1–12.

In Mary Hoffman's story *The Three Wise Women* (it's a children's book, beautifully illustrated and suitable for any age!), three women follow a star and bring their own distinctive gifts to the child. One woman, the eldest of the three, brings the gift of stories. She tells stories to a baby who when he grows up will tell the most wonderful stories to anyone who listens. When the women return to their villages, no one has noticed that they have been away and no one remembers the star they followed.

● Why is the gift of stories significant?

Think about the wonder of stories: how they need to be known, loved and told. What is it we express when we share stories?

Tell some of your own stories now.

New Beginnings

Ask one of the group to read this story by Rev Linda Bandelier:

> *One Sunday when I was 19 years old, living far from home, I went to church and met Clare. After the service she said, 'Let's go to breakfast.'*
>
> *As we left the church I mentally counted all the money that wasn't in my pocket.*

Think about the wonder of stories: how they need to be known, loved and told

At the café I ordered the cheapest item on the menu.

'Is that all you want?!' asked Clare.

'To tell the truth, I don't have any money. I can't pay you back.'

'Order what you want.'

After breakfast and much conversation I said again, 'I don't have any money. I can't pay you back.'

Clare said, 'Let me tell you a story. When I was about your age I had nothing. I needed a home, money, food and work. A couple took me in. They gave me a home, fed me and helped me find a job. They helped me until I could manage on my own. One day I said to them, "I can never repay you." They said, "We know, but someday you will pass this on." Linda, I didn't invite you because I knew you could pay. Some day you will pass this on.'

Think about re-discovering the joy and power of telling and re-telling our stories, how each telling is a new birth.

Towards a conclusion

Nobody, but nobody, was paying attention. Her arguments were sound, her ideas compelling, her phrasings striking. But her speech was falling on stony ground. No one was taking any interest. She paused. 'Once upon a time,' she said, starting again. Suddenly everyone was quiet, everyone was listening.

'Once upon a time, the Prime Minister of India went for a walk with a swallow and an eel.' She had them all now, she knew, in the palm of her hand.

(Angela Wood and Robin Richardson, from Inside Stories, *Trentham Books, 1992)*

'Once upon a time...'

PRAYER

God of our imaginings, help us to re-dream the world through the stories we tell.

ACTION

Look more deeply into stories and story-telling. These books will help: *Three Wise Women* by Mary Hoffman illustrated by Lynne Russell, published by Frances

Lincoln, 1999; or *Inside Stories* by Angela Wood and Robin Richardson. Contact a professional story-teller. Rev Linda Bandelier, singer, songwriter and story-teller, may be contacted at 30 Newhaven Road, Edinburgh EH6 5PY, Scotland.

Study 2 *Somebody Touched me*

AIM

To look at threshold experiences and challenge taboos.

PREPARATION

Ask two or three members of the group to be prepared to take part in a reading and mime of the two stories in Luke 8.40–56. Think carefully about what is going to happen and prepare well. You are working with stories (rather than poetry) so without care the mime could easily become over-dramatic. Mime is meditative, using movements and gestures to encourage reflection and understanding with our whole being. Emotions may be expressed in a look, in a touch. Try to talk together about the mime before the whole group meets.

Thresholds

The folk who have prepared read and mime Luke 8.40–48. Then read:

Woman with Bleeding

Shalom: an end to exclusion.
Now, not he the miracle-worker
but she, daughter of the people,
is heroine in her story.

She no longer laments
blood staining her living;
lifeblood flowing from her
like children unborn.

For healing is happening
in their bodies.
The living energy of touch
liberates woman and man
to go out in wholeness:

Keynote readings
Luke 8.40–48
Luke 8.49–56

The living
energy
of touch
liberates
woman
and man

a brave and rounded humanity;
free; to be called divine.
(Joy Mead)

Be still and silent for a few minutes.

Continue to read and mime Luke 8.49–56, followed by:

Jairus' Daughter

'Get up, my child!'
this is no time for sleeping.
Lighter than Lazarus,
this raising; his touch
an affirmation of womanhood
amid the misted familiar.

Flute players re-tune
to celebrate the coming
of her bleeding, and the chance
between waxing and waning
of moons, for new life.

Mother and father watch,
unable to do anything
but offer wholesome food
for the journey.
The threshold is hers
to cross alone; her knowing
is outside theirs
in the shadow of the unsaid.
(Joy Mead)

Remain still and quiet for a few minutes.

What do you think is happening in these stories? Why do they lend themselves so well to mime?

Do the remains of ... taboos live on today in our silences?

Have you ever heard in a sermon or Bible study that the woman had a menstrual disorder or that Jairus' daughter had reached the age of puberty and begun menstruating?

Why is the offering of food so significant? Has the girl been refusing food, delaying the threshold crossing into womanhood?

When the woman touched Jesus and Jesus touched the girl, taboos of the day were broken; there was healing. Do the remains of these taboos live on today in our silences – in the things we won't talk about? What are the possibilities for health and wholeness if the silence were broken – if we told a different story?

People have a fear of not being in control. When our bodies go wrong, or change, we feel powerless. What do you think these stories say to us about control?

Towards a conclusion
If your life has gone wrong you need to take from others, to touch freely, not to feel that you are taboo. Wholeness is not something individual. All people we reach out to touch, or who reach out to touch us, influence our will to wholeness. In this touching is the potential for resurrection. These stories do not call for faith in miracles we know can't happen but for taboo-breaking touch which makes us whole again and gives us faith in ourselves.

PRAYER

Feel for the people we most avoid,
Strange or bereaved or never employed;
Feel for the women, and feel for the men
Who fear that their living is all in vain.

To the lost Christ shows his face;
To the unloved he gives his embrace;
To those who cry in pain or disgrace,
Christ makes, with his friends, a touching place.
(John Bell, from Love from Below, *Wild Goose Publications)*

Feel for
the people
we most avoid

ACTION

Find out more about attitudes to illness that are socially exclusive. Look for signs of hope: contact **Ethiopiaid**, Bedford House, Madeira Walk, Windsor SL4 1EU, and ask about the Addis Ababa Fistula Hospital that gives back life to women who are often social outcasts.

NOTES BY VAL
OGDEN

MORE GOSPEL STORIES FOR TODAY

Study 1 *Stones, Wine and Water*

Keynote readings
John 8.1–11
John 4.7–18, 27–30
John 2.1–12

AIM

To encounter three different women in John's Gospel who point us towards truths about Jesus.

Setting

Write out the following references on separate pieces of coloured paper or card. Lay out the cards where everyone can see them and place an appropriate symbol on each.

● John 8.1–11: a few pebbles;

● John 4. 7–18 & 27–30: drinking water in a glass;

● John 2.1–12: a bottle of wine and a wine glass.

Questions and method

Each Bible passage features an encounter between Jesus and a particular woman. The encounters are recorded by the writer of John in the hope that we will read the lines and read behind the lines with imagination. To help the group to do this, ask them to hold in their minds three questions as they listen to the stories:

● Who is this woman?

● Who is this woman in Jesus' eyes?

● What truths about Jesus does this woman help us to understand?

Who is this woman?

Ask for each passage to be read aloud, even if people are following it in their own Bibles. Then encourage discussion around the questions. Creative suggestions are offered below for each reading. However, these are not to be interpreted as the 'right answers'. Encourage members to engage with the stories for themselves and think freely.

Who is this woman?

John 8.1–11: A wily adulteress? An unfortunate victim? Sad? Sinful? A law breaker?

| John 4.7–18, 27–30: | An 'unclean' foreigner? A woman carrying out the daily drudgery of drawing water? A loose woman with a reputation? |
| John 2.1–12: | A proud mother? A domineering, annoying mother? An anxious guest? |

Who is this woman in Jesus' eyes?

John 8.1–11:	Another source of dispute between himself and the teachers of the Law? A sinner who needs forgiveness? A victim who needs justice?
John 4.7–18, 27–30:	Someone to give him a drink? An arrogant questioner? An amateur theologian? An immoral woman who needs correction?
John 2.1–12:	A beloved parent? A fussy mother? Someone who needs correction?

What truths about Jesus does this woman help us to understand?

John 8.1–11:	Jesus' refusal to live by the letter of the Law? Jesus' concern for justice and compassion? Jesus as saviour not judge?
John 4.7–18, 27–30:	Jesus' availability to all? Jesus as the source of eternal life? Jesus' new attitude towards women? Jesus as Messiah?
John 2.1–12:	Jesus has God-given powers? Jesus is to be obeyed? Jesus' way will be 'new wine' for the world?

PRAYER

Pick up the handful of pebbles and give thanks for an insight shared from the John 8 reading.

Pick up the glass of water and give thanks for an insight shared from the John 4 reading

Pick up the bottle and wine glass and give thanks for an insight shared from the John 2 reading.

'Sir ... you have no bucket and the well is deep...'
John 4.11, REB

ACTION

Have you read about, listened to or watched on video real-life stories of how Jesus has affected the lives of 20th or 21st century women? Find a good one through your local Christian bookshop or your Church's publishing house. Enjoy it and then share it.

Study 2 *Wholly Fasting – Holy Feasting*

Keynote readings
Luke 5.33–6.5
Luke 12.22–29

AIM

To explore what fasting and feasting might mean in our Christian lives today, with the help of two sections from Luke's Gospel.

Opening activity

Encourage participants to talk about a memorable 'feast' they were part of, e.g. a wedding reception, a family meal to celebrate a birthday or anniversary, dining out with friends, or a picnic in the open air. Look at menus and photographs if possible so that people have a real 'taste' of the occasions being described.

'Have you not read what David did when he and his men were hungry?'

Luke 6.3, REB

Read Luke 5.33 – 6.5. If possible use different people to read the parts: people, Jesus, Pharisees.

Talk about the two objections raised about the disciples' eating habits:

5.33 they seem to enjoy their food and drink, which doesn't seem correct when compared to other 'holy' people.

6.2 they satisfy their own hunger at the expense of the Sabbath law.

Discuss

● When have you been made to feel guilty about eating and drinking?

● Who or what made you feel guilty and was it justified?

● How do you draw the line between feasting and indulgence?

Read Luke 12.22–31. Wrestle with the following tough questions, which have no set answers...

Verses 22 and 29: How can this teaching be appropriate for a mother in the developing world struggling to find daily food for her children?

Verses 30 and 31: How can someone with an empty stomach be concerned with the Kingdom?

Share this story – Lilian Mwansa's diary – Zambia

Monday

6.30am I pick the last of the tomatoes and green vegetables from my yard, put the baby on my back, and walk one hour to the big market on the outskirts of town. Three children have remained at home. Their big brother, my first-born, has gone to school. I have managed to pay fees for him but not for the others. Today we had enough maize meal to eat porridge for breakfast, but now it has finished. They will only eat mangoes from the tree for lunch.

12.00 noon The market is busy today – the whole world has something to sell but only a few come to buy. My friend who sits in the space next to me has also brought tomatoes and green vegetables to sell. Her tomatoes have fewer black marks and are firmer so she sells more. By 5.00pm I have only enough money to buy maize for tonight's meal and for breakfast tomorrow. My friend has sold enough to buy beans. She scoops four handfuls of them into my sack. Thank you so much, my sister. God is kind!

7.30pm The children will cook beans tomorrow. It will take too long to cook them on the charcoal fire tonight and we are hungry. My eldest daughter cooks the maize and brings it to the table with the green vegetables that I failed to sell, and some dry fish. 'Mummy, we sold some mangoes at the gate,' she tells me, 'so we bought fish with the money.' 'You did well, my daughter.' We pray and eat. Who would have believed we would sleep with full stomachs tonight? But that is how the Lord provides for his children. God is kind!

Discuss reactions to this story. How does God provide for you in your circumstances?

Food for body and soul...

17

Break bread together

Pass around something simple, like a fruit loaf and a large mug of juice; breaking the loaf and sharing the drink one with the next. Gentle music can be played on tape as this is being done and a simple prayer of thanksgiving for God's provision can be shared at the end.

ACTION

Commit yourself in the near future to either a fast or a feast – or both.

Fast for a day, on your own or as a group, and donate the money you would have spent on food to a charity such as Christian Aid.

Invite one or two people who've never been to your home to come and share a meal so that you can enjoy preparing food for them and feasting together.

PSALMS FOR TODAY

Study 1 *Digging Below the Surface*

AIM

To see how far the psalms we are looking at speak to situations we ourselves face, living under very different conditions – or are the conditions so very different?

Way in

Read together Psalm 33, a great hymn of confident praise, and then spend a few moments quietly thinking about what you have read.

Good and evil, law and freedom

Now to look a little closer at some of the questions we might want to ask. Psalm 1 draws a sharp contrast between the wicked and the righteous and stresses that the righteous 'delight in the law of the Lord.' All too often God's law has been portrayed as defining in great detail what should or should not be done in such a way as to leave us in a no-win situation. However, law here should be understood as guidelines or teaching, the means by which God leads us into the fuller, richer way of life; and if we go on to see that teaching actually embodied in life in Jesus, things can look quite different.

● What examples would head your list of wickedness in the world we know today? Do you think they are greatly different from those activities which the Psalmist may have had in mind?

● There is a great emphasis today on individual rights and freedom. From a Christian perspective what do you see as the relationship between law – in particular 'the law of the Lord' – and freedom?

● Jesus taught that the supreme commandment was that we should love God and the second that we should love our neighbour (*e.g. Mark 12.29–31*). If all else in the law

Keynote readings
Psalm 1
Psalm 2
Psalm 6
Psalm 29
Psalm 33
Psalm 34.1–10

*If we go on to
see teaching
actually
embodied
in life in Jesus,
things can look
quite different*

19

*Show favour
to me, Lord,
for my strength
fails*
Psalm 6.2, REB

of God hangs on these two, how do you interpret them? How far do they influence the way you live?

- If the righteousness of God is shown in the ways the Almighty does right by the weak and oppressed *(e.g. Psalm 34.6)*, how should we interpret the call to righteousness in our own lives?

Will good prevail over evil?

We get a number of expressions of confidence that evil will be thwarted and good will prevail *(e.g. Psalms 1.6, 2.4, 33.10, 34.10)* but also an awareness of times when evil appears to be triumphing *(e.g. Psalm 6)*.

- Do you believe good will always triumph eventually?

- In this context how are we to understand the cross of Christ?

- Is making every effort to do what we believe is right its own reward, or do we depend upon a future judgement to even the scores?

Experiencing the goodness of the Lord

There are many expressions of praise and thanksgiving for the goodness of God, including such confident claims as 'those who seek the Lord lack no good thing' *(Psalm 34.10, REB)*. Yet in Psalm 6.1–7 we have an anguished cry from the heart in a time of pain and weakness.

Share some instances you know of faithful worshippers who have to battle with pain, disability or sorrow. Does God send these troubles, do you think? How are we to understand God's care for those who suffer in this way?

- Do you feel that you have personally experienced the 'goodness of the Lord?'

- Is it possible to 'taste the goodness of the Lord' even when our lives are falling apart?

An inconclusive conclusion?

You may feel that your discussions have left some questions still unanswered. If so, take comfort from the fact that that has been the experience of deeply committed Christians across the ages, for though we must use our minds to the full and ask searching questions if we are truly to serve God, there are also times when we can only journey in faith.

PRAYER

Finish by reading together Psalm 36.5–10 and then, after a short period for quiet reflection, say the Grace together.

ACTION

Make a little time to consider what it means for your day-to-day living that God's call to us is not so much to *be* right, to *be* good, as to *do* right, to *do* good.

Study 2 *Digging Further*

AIM

To look at further psalms, especially noting what they have to say about wider relationships within the nation – and beyond.

Way in

Discuss briefly the events which are making national and international headlines at the moment. This is our world; the context in which we are asking what these psalms may have to say to us.

God is our shelter

'God is our shelter and strength, always ready to help in time of trouble'. This is the Good News Bible translation of Psalm 46.1. The psalm pictures the world in turmoil, but in the midst of all the upheaval is a haven, 'the city of God'.

● Our own world is no less in turmoil; can we have the same confidence that we find expressed in this psalm?

● Where, would you say, might we find the secure haven, the 'city of God'?

● The psalmist was thinking of a place, but is it also possible to carry something of this sense of security within us, to know we are safe, whatever happens, because we belong to the city, are citizens, even though we are in a 'foreign land'?

Keynote readings
Psalm 46
Psalm 71.1–6
Psalm 72
Psalm 96
Psalm 135
Psalm 138
Psalm 147.12–20

God is our shelter and strength
Psalm 46.1, REB

A prayer for good government

Psalm 72 is essentially a prayer for good government which can well be translated from the Kingdom of Israel under Solomon to the present day. The Psalm opens with 'Teach the king to judge with your righteousness, O God'. and verses 12–14 give some idea of what the psalmist has in mind.

● How far do you think the laws that govern life in your country reflect the laws of God, the righteousness of God?

Are religion and politics two separate worlds?

● Are religion and politics two separate worlds, or do you think Christians have a duty openly to encourage or criticize their government in the light of their own understanding of what the Lord requires?

● Do you think Christians should be more involved in politics or less?

A God of all peoples?

Psalm 135 is a great hymn of praise, but verses 8–11 show that the Almighty is seen as a God who is expected to help one group of people at the expense of others. The theme is repeated in Psalm 147. In much of the Old Testament this is taken for granted and it has also affected quite a lot of thinking in the Christian Church.

● Does God care only for a select community, be it Jewish, Christian, Muslim or what you will, or is his loving care for the whole of humanity?

● If God is indeed the God of all, how should this affect our relationships with Christians of other traditions? People of other faiths? People of no faith?

Bring an offering...

In verse 8 of Psalm 96 we read, 'bring an offering and come into his courts'.

We are used to making a gift of money when the plate is passed round in the course of worship, but take time to consider afresh what might be the offering the Lord is looking for you to bring in daily life.

PRAYER

Thank you, Lord, for strength to match our weakness,
comfort to lighten our distress,
guidance to lead us in perplexity,
inner peace to hold us against disaster,
love to dissolve our bitterness
and forgiveness to cover our failure.
So much has been given to us.
Show us how we may share your gifts
with others in their time of need.

ACTION

Try composing a prayer for your own land and for its politicians and administrators; your own prayer for good government.

NOTES BY
JOY MEAD

DARE TO BE DIFFERENT

Study 1 *Live Simply*

Keynote readings
Matthew 11.25–30
Jeremiah 17.5–10
Luke 12.32–34

AIM

To develop our understanding of living simply as dancing lightly on the earth.

PREPARATION

If possible, have available a recording of Aaron Copland's ballet suite Appalachian Spring. *Play it quietly as people arrive, concentrating on the section which includes the Shaker melody* Simple Gifts *(easily recognized as the basis for* Lord of the Dance*).*

'When true simplicity is gained'
Read together Matthew 11.25–30.

The Shakers saw themselves as people setting a new example and redefining what the good life is. They were daring to be different, renouncing wealth, living lightly. Read together the words of the Shaker song *Simple Gifts*:

'Tis the gift to be simple, 'tis the gift to be free,
'Tis the gift to come down where we ought to be,
And when we find ourselves in the place just right
'Twill be in the valley of love and delight.

When true simplicity is gained
To bow and to bend we shan't be ashamed;
To turn, turn will be our delight
Till by turning, turning we come round right.

- What do you think is revealed to the simple?
- What is it that leads to the gaining of true simplicity?
- Is it to do with 'the place just right', being ourselves 'till by turning, turning we come round right'?
- Is the basis of our true welfare: where community life is rich, air is clean, there's always work to do and the good things are shared?

Aaron Copland's ballet suite *Appalachian Spring* includes the traditional Shaker melody *Simple Gifts* as the theme for a set of variations. The ballet centres on the celebration in spring of a newly-built farmhouse in the Pennsylvania hills in the early part of the 19th century. It opens with a Revivalist Preacher, a Pioneer Woman experienced in the ways of the wilderness, a young Husbandman, his bride and a group of four women followers of the Preacher entering in turn. After a general dance, the followers pray together then the Revivalist leads an extended dance. The dance to the melody *Simple Gifts* is performed by the husbandman and his bride when they are left quiet and strong in their new house.

Think about what is happening in the ballet story and the idea of 'the place just right'.

Lord of the Dance
Now, with the Shaker melody still in mind – playing quietly if possible – read together Sydney Carter's *Lord of the Dance*. Sydney Carter sometimes suggests singing the whole song in the present tense: 'I dance in the morning when the world is begun…' Try it. Ask the group what difference it makes to them.

Sydney Carter talks of 'singing … the dancing pattern in the life and words of Jesus.' Think about words and music – and dancing – the way dancing unites physical and spiritual. Many Christians have thought of dancing as a bit frivolous. The Shakers didn't. They thought of dancing as a simple spiritual activity. They also made furniture with the same beautiful lyrical simplicity – uniting material and spiritual.

'I dance in the morning when the world is begun'

Towards a conclusion

The words from Matthew 11.25–30 *(also in Luke 10.21–22)* are thanksgiving for revelation. Do you see what is revealed to the simple as the treasure: the gift of life itself; finding our humanness and being true to it? Living simply doesn't mean being poor, it means walking lightly on our earth caring for and respecting all with which we share it.

PRAYER

Vulnerable God,
give us:
sensibility: that we may learn to think fragility;
understanding: that we may know our part
in the intricate pattern of being;
companionship: that we may live gently and simply
alongside all living things
simplicity: that we may dance lightly
on the good earth.

ACTION

Look again at this week's key readings. You will see that they are all 'dares': to live simply, to be a peacemaker, to resist consumerism and the pressure of 'The Market'. Take up the dares: be different.

Study 2 *Be Peacemakers*

Keynote readings
Luke 6.27–31
Luke 6.32–36

AIM

To understand peace as a pathway we make, not an end we travel towards.

PREPARATION

Cut out large pebble shapes – suitable to have words written on in big letters and to make a pathway – and give one to each member of the group as he or she arrives.

Compassion,
co-operation,
community and
companionship

Words of Peace

Read together Luke 6.32–36, thinking particularly about verse 36. Compassion, co-operation, community and companionship with mutual respect, inclusiveness and sharing are what build the way of peace.

● What do you think compassion means? Do you see it as an integral part of peacemaking?

In his Bible reading notes on this passage for *Words for Today*, John Morrow from the Corrymeela Community writes of 'digging deeper to find firmer foundations based on mutual respect, the participation of all and a more equal sharing of resources' (February 24).

● What do you think 'digging deeper' means? Does it involve making ourselves vulnerable?

Keep a few minutes' silence to ponder the answers to these questions.

Now say together this *Meditation on Peace*:

Peace is not a thing to possess, but a way of possessing;
Peace is not a gift to be given, but a way of giving;
Peace is not a topic to teach, but a way of teaching;
Peace is not a theory to learn, but a way of learning;
Peace is not an opinion to hold, but a way of holding;
Peace is not a resolution of strife, but a way of striving;
Peace is not a creed to preach, but a way of preaching;
Peace is not a God to serve, but a way of serving;
Peace is not a question to ask, but a way of asking;
Peace is not an answer to seek, but a way of seeking;
Peace is not a journey's end, but a way of journeying.
(Richard Skinner, from Prayers for Peacemakers,
Kevin Mayhew Publishers, 1988)

Peace is not a journey's end, but a way of journeying

Ask members of the group to write peace words on their pebbles then make a pathway with them. Look at the words. Are there common elements – for example, can the words be separated into the personal and political aspects of peace?

● Are the words of your path active or passive?

Keep a few moments' silence as you look at your path.

Read together these words by John Bell of the Iona Community:

Enemy of Apathy

She sits like a bird, brooding on the waters,
Hovering on the chaos of the world's first day;
She sighs and she sings, mothering creation,
Waiting to give birth to all the Word will say.

She wings over earth, resting where she wishes,
Lighting close at hand or soaring through the skies;
She nests in the womb, welcoming each wonder,
Nourishing potential hidden to our eyes.

She dances in fire, startling her spectators,
Waking tongues of ecstasy where dumbness reigned;
She weans and inspires all whose hearts are open,
Nor can she be captured, silenced or restrained.

For she is the Spirit, one with God in essence,
Gifted by the Saviour in eternal love;
She is the key opening the scriptures,
Enemy of apathy and heavenly dove.

Think about how many of the words about peace are *verbs* – active or doing words.

Towards a conclusion
'My peace I leave with you' – not to lull but to inspire you.

Peace is not passivity or inactivity; it's about making. Drama, painting, craft, creative listening – co-operative activities – are peacemaking activities.

Take our prejudices and make them into peace offerings...

PRAYER

Take our hatreds: make them into handshakes
Take our prejudices: make them into peace-offerings
Take our arguments: make them into alliances
Take our battles: make them into bonds
Take our misunderstandings: make them into music
Take our divisions: make them into dances
Take our schisms: make them into songs
(*Kate Compston, from* Textures of Tomorrow,
The United Reformed Church, 1996)

ACTION

Be active for peace. Contact the Peace Pledge Union. Find out about the Campaign Against the Arms Trade. Encourage thinking about peacemaking as a central part of worship.

Study 3 *Let God be Seen in You*

AIM

To explore the meaning of goodness.

Keynote readings
2 Corinthians 3.23–4.2
Isaiah 58.1–12

PREPARATION

Ask each member of the group to bring a picture of the face of a good person.

Let the light shine through

Begin by reading together 2 Corinthians 3.23–4.2 and Isaiah 58.1–12.

Together, look at your pictures and tell their stories. As you do so, hold particularly in mind the words from Isaiah (verse 8): 'Your light will break forth like the dawn…'

Endeavour to discover what makes these people good, what quality of life shines through. Good people are difficult to define – but we know them when we see them.

Good people are difficult to define – but we know them when we see them

Even in modern life kindness and generosity continue to be valued; where does the innate capacity for goodness in so many men and women come from? Does goodness demand invisibility; like the person who waits without making things happen, without interfering but with a quiet love that asks nothing for itself? Are there people like that amongst your examples? Is goodness more than that?

Look again at the words of Isaiah and Paul. Is this all more about our humanness and our openness to the Spirit? Is it more to do with availability than perfection? Does openness to the Spirit help us to enjoy one another's faces?

Think quietly for a few moments about what this really means.

Read together:

Marked man

*He bears the marks of suffering
on his flesh and on his soul.*

*The white-hot fire that leaps and soars,
roaring like a lion through steamy jungles*

and dark, long-walled ravines,
emerald-eyed and glittering;
or flickers delicately, casting dreams and shadows
in tall pillars ascending to blue heavens;
this fire chars and crumbles
smoking, scorching,
choking into barren blackness,
empty night.

A cold starlight glimmers,
A peal of bells sings out across green land.
A spring of running water mirrors flame.

He carries woundedness precisely,
neither denying
nor idolizing,
only recognizing.

To me, he is beautiful.
He is who he is.
To me he is beautiful.

(*Kathy Galloway, from* Talking to the Bones, *SPCK, 1996*)

This is a face to enjoy; a face that enables us to glimpse God. Why?

Think about meeting someone loved and longed for in a busy place – searching out the face. When we look into the face we will recognize more than the loved one – we will begin to recognize what we're really like. 'However damaged, hurt, abused your body, you remain God's dwelling place and home' (Donald Eadie, *Grain in Winter*, Epworth Press, 1999). Is this what being human really means?

Openness to the Spirit is part of what makes us whole and wholly human. It brings an awareness of that deep part of us that is neither divisive nor exclusive but responds to all life with love, joy, peace and justice.

Think about being still and looking at people, things, events. Is it the looking that saves us? Does the light by which we look shine through us (rather than on us)?

Towards a conclusion

'At times I meet able, competent people who live their lives surrounded by the ambitious, in an achievement-, success-oriented culture, and they refuse to play the

Is it the looking that saves us? Does the light by which we look shine through us rather than on us?

game, refuse to push others out of the way as they climb ladders. Instead they choose to remain where they are, listening, caring, working at depths, making a testimony to humanity in what can at times be a brutal crucible. And some will call this foolishness!'

(Donald Eadie, from Grain in Winter, *Epworth Press, 1999)*

● What do you call it?

PRAYER

May God be seen in the fullness of our humanity: in the way we see and understand; the way we attend to the minutest things: stones, spoons, flowers, tiny gestures.

ACTION

Look at ordinary everyday things, faces; explore the possibilities; celebrate the here and now, and lives and people within it; encourage others to do the same.

JOURNEYING WITH CHRIST

Notes for the Leader

Provide a candle large enough to last eight weeks, notebooks and pens. Set up tapes or CDs beforehand. Do not turn them on or off suddenly; always fade music in and out.

Study 1 *Which Way?*

Keynote readings
Luke 4.1–13
Luke 9.57–62
Luke 11.29–32

AIM

To see where we have come from.

PREPARATION

- *The candle;*
- *Stones and small cactus placed by the candle;*
- *A picture to represent 'bleakness' (Colour supplements are a good source, or invest in a set of postcards from the Methodist Art Collection [Methodist Publishing House, 01733 332202]);*
- *Music set ready to use – perhaps* Andante in C Major K315, Romantic Music for Flute and Harp *(Mozart);*
- *People may like notebooks handy.*

Welcome

In the next eight weeks we will be travelling together. We will be asking ourselves who we are and where we are going. Maybe we think we know one another pretty well already. Perhaps this means we have to listen especially carefully.

- Take time for people to chat generally about how long they have known one another. Where did they first meet? How did they become part of this group? During the conversation light a candle in the centre.

The wilderness

When you feel it is time, draw the conversation to a close. Allow people to settle down. Perhaps someone would like to describe an arid landscape in a country they have visited. Refer to the stones and the cactus. Show the picture which suggests bleakness to you. Pass it round. Place it by the candle. Suggest that members might like to focus on the stones or the cactus or the picture, or close their eyes.

Speak slowly and clearly:

We are thinking of a time when our own lives have felt hard or uncomfortable. Allow your mind to travel back over your life ... (*allow some time*) ... Maybe there were times when things felt pretty bleak? ... (*allow some time*) ... (*after a while, quietly throw in suggestions*) ... Maybe the children were all small and you had no transport ... Maybe money was short ... Maybe someone was very ill ... Maybe you had too much do ... Maybe you didn't have enough to do....

Put on the music.

● Sit quietly with the music; suggest that people bring those times to mind.

● Suggest that people might find it helpful to jot down an example of a time when things felt bleak, either just for themselves or to share with someone nearby.

● Invite members to share one of the bleak times with a neighbour ... or to be willing to listen to someone else's experience ... or to sit quietly.

● If people are talking to one another, give them time to finish. Very quiet music could continue.

● If people are not talking, move on.

● Point out that people in the group have had their own wilderness experiences.

Jesus' wilderness experience
Read Luke 4.1–13 slowly. Encourage people to shut their eyes and to imagine the scene. After the reading ask some quiet questions ... maybe:

● Is the landscape stony or sandy?

● Can you feel the heat?

● What is the expression on Jesus' face?

● How do you think he feels?

Allow a few moments to 'wake up', then talk about what was imagined.

We are thinking of a time when our own lives have felt hard or uncomfortable

Read the last verses again ... Jesus moved on.

Pull me through

> *Pull me through, dear God –*
> *just pull me through*
> *once more,*
> *because I'm stuck and*
> *it's dark, dear God just give me*
> *a little pull,*
> *Because there is no space*
> *down here*
> *and I cannot see the sky.*
> *Just give me*
> *a little pull, dear God –*
> *only a little pull,*
> *for I want to smell the morning rain*
> *and feel the cold,*
> *free breeze.*
> *Oh, give me a little pull,*
> *dear God,*
> *just a little pull.*

(Edwina Gateley, from There was no path so I trod one, *Source Books, Box 794 Trabuco Canyon, CA 92678 USA)*

- What or who had allowed members of the group to move on?
- Suggest that people chat in twos.
- Remember some people are still in the wilderness ... or never quite free of it.

ACTION

As a group or as individuals identify people in your communities who are stuck in the wilderness. Are there carers who have no other life, lone parents or people who suffer from depression, and their families? Perhaps you can share ideas of how you might be able to help. Pray for these people.

PRAYER

> *Lord, forgive our preoccupation*
> *with all that is less than essential.*
> *Dare us to follow you by asking true questions.*

There was no path so I trod one

Study 2 *The Cost*

AIM

To consider what it means to be a disciple.

PREPARATION

Keynote readings
Jeremiah 22.1–9, 13–17
Luke 14.25–33
2 Timothy 2.1–13
Philippians 3.12–21

- *The candle, stones, cactus and picture from last week. You will need a space cleared to move them later.*
- *Look up 'disciple' in a dictionary. Write the definition in the middle of a large sheet of paper or a white board.*
- *Have pens available.*
- *You might like to photocopy THE MESSAGE version of the Bible passage for everyone.*
- *Have quiet music set at the right place: perhaps* Symphony 5, The Adagio *(Mahler).*
- *A recent news story about the persecution of Christians*
- *Give next session's Bible reading to someone to prepare.*

Welcome

Have the unlit candle, stones, cactus and picture already arranged as before. As people arrive, encourage some general chat about last week. When everyone has arrived, suggest that people might like to share, in twos or threes, any thoughts that have followed on from last week. If any particular concerns or issues have emerged, talk them over all together for a few minutes.

Light the candle.

Prayer

In silence ... we think about the people beside us ... and we pray...

Stay with us, Lord; kindle our hearts on the way, that we may recognize you in the Scriptures, in the breaking of bread and in each other, for you love and guide us for ever. Amen

Stay with us, Lord; kindle our hearts on the way

Paul's journey with Christ

Read, as dramatically as possible, the following version of Philippians 3.12–21 (or use another version if you prefer, of course):

I'm not saying that I have this all together, that I have it made. But I am well on my way, reaching out for Christ, who has so wondrously reached out for me. Friends, don't get me wrong: By no means do I count myself an expert in all of this, but I've got my eye on the goal, where God is beckoning us onward – to Jesus. I'm off and running, and I'm not turning back.

So let's keep focused on that goal, those of us who want everything God has for us. If any of you have something else in mind, something less than total commitment, God will clear your blurred vision – you'll see it yet! Now that we're on the right track, let's stay on it.

Stick with me, friends. Keep track of those you see running this same course, headed for this same goal. There are many out there taking other paths, choosing other goals, and trying to get you to go along with them. I've warned you of them many times; sadly, I'm having to do it again. All they want is easy street. They hate Christ's Cross. But easy street is a dead-end street. Those who live there make their bellies their gods; belches are their praise; all they can think of is their appetites.

He'll make us beautiful and whole

But there's far more to life for us. We're citizens of high heaven! We're waiting the arrival of the Saviour, the Master, Jesus Christ, who will transform our earthy bodies into glorious bodies like his own. He'll make us beautiful and whole with the same powerful skill by which he is putting everything as it should be, under and around him.

(From THE MESSAGE, © Eugene Peterson.
Used by permission of NavPress Publishing Group)

Follow this with a short silence.

- Chat to your neighbour about how that passage leaves you feeling.
- If there are people who feel daunted, maybe they could share their feelings with the group.
- Those who feel encouraged could also share their feelings.
- Emphasize that we are talking about our feelings. They are not right or wrong.

Allow some time for sharing of ideas.

How do we journey with Christ?

Move the candle, stones, cactus and picture to their cleared space. Place the very large piece of paper on the floor. Point out the meanings of 'disciple'. Explain where you found them. Do any of these meanings describe us? Followers of a leader ... a teacher.

● Say that you are going to gather together as much of the teaching of Jesus as you have time or space for. For example... 'Blessed are the meek' ... 'Give all you have to the poor' ... 'Turn the other cheek' ... 'Love your enemies' ... 'Love one another' ... 'Forgive your brother seventy times seven'. Give one example and see how it goes. Write the phrases round the definition of 'disciple'. Get people to stick to the teaching of Jesus. Add others as you go from your own list if necessary.

When you have finished, ask people to sit back. Start the music and speak the phrases slowly and clearly over the music with a pause between each... Finish with a little music.

● Is this how we are to live as we journey with Christ?

● Are they an easy set of guidelines?

● How do we feel?

● Allow a short time to chat about it.

The journey is costly

Tell or read a recent story of persecuted Christians. Share stories for a short while.

● Do we have examples from our own community?

Place the lit candle and the stone on one corner of the paper. Place the cross on the opposite corner. Explain that we are remembering all those who are persecuted. We are thinking of other people and of ourselves who are trying to journey with Christ and finding it difficult.

Read with two voices:

The Way

Friend, I have lost the way.

The way leads on.

The way leads on

The way is one

Is there another way?
The way is one.
I must retrace the track.
It's lost and gone.
Back, I must travel back!
None goes there, none.
Then I'll make here my place,
(The road runs on),
Stand still and set my face,
(The road leaps on),
Stay here, for ever stay.
None stays here, none.
I cannot find the way.
The way leads on.
Oh places I have passed!
That journey's done.
And what will come at last?
The road leads on.

(Edwin Muir, from *Collected Poems*, Faber & Faber, 1960)

ACTION

Identify one way in which your church does not reflect the teaching of Jesus and do something about it. Give extra encouragement and support to young people in your church community.

PRAYER

When we know that others are walking in the darkness give us courage to be light for them.

Blow out the candle.

Study 3 *Time for God*

Keynote readings
Isaiah 55.1–9
Genesis 28.10–19a
1 Corinthians 10.1–13
John 1.43–51
Matthew 6.7–15
John 15.1–10

AIM

To consider what we mean by 'time for God'.

PREPARATION

- *The candle, stones and picture;*
- *Last week's sheet of paper;*
- *Your kitchen calendar;*
- *Your diary;*
- *Music – anything from Pergolesi's Stabat Mater;*

- *A4 paper;*
- *Felt-tipped pens.*

Welcome

Have the 'teachings of Jesus' paper in the middle of the circle when people arrive. The candle is in the centre with the other objects. Encourage chat about last week's time together and the conversations around the objects. When everyone has arrived and settled down, light the candle.

Remind people that last time some found it daunting to journey with Christ. Others were challenged. Allow a few minutes' general talk. Suggest that in either case it can be difficult to accept that doing nothing is an important part of our journey.

Place your calendar or diary near the candle. Suggest that others might do the same. Encourage people to take off their watches and put them round the candle too. If there are people who feel that they have too much time because of age or ill health or unemployment, encourage them to talk about it.

'If you heed my commands you will dwell in love'
John 15,10, REB

Prayer

Sit quietly. Speak slowly, and count silently up to at least five after each line:

Be silent
Be still.
Alone. Empty
before your God.
Say nothing
Ask nothing.
Be silent.
Be still.
Let your God
look upon you.
That is all.
God knows
God understands.
God loves you with an enormous love.
God only wants to
look upon you with love.
Quiet
Still
Be.

(*Edwina Gateley, from* Psalms of a Laywoman, *reprinted by permission of Sheed & Ward, an Apostolate of the Priests of the*

Sacred Heart, 7373 South Lover's Lane Road, Franklin, Wisconsin 53132)

Stay silent for a few moments, then say together:

Amen

● What feelings does the prayer arouse in you?

● Finding the time to *be* is difficult. For others *doing* is difficult.

Today we are reminding ourselves that *being* is an important part of our time for God.

Read Matthew 6.7–15.

● Suggest that prayer is a time to get on God's wavelength.

● Does the group agree?

Have each person write a short sentence about prayer on an A4 sheet and put it on the floor for everyone to read. Then each one should pick up someone else's sheet and say what he or she finds helpful in it.

About this Bible passage

Ask people to listen. Start the music, and say clearly and slowly: 'Your father knows what you need before you ask him.'

● What feelings does this arouse?

Love needs time ... a story from Wanda Hayman

A friend of mine was married to the kindest man I ever met. They loved each other and worked together for the church. One thing, however, clouded the skies – her husband, busy as a minister, very seldom made any time for her and their son. For fifteen years she loyally persuaded herself that he really wasn't able to find time for them. But suddenly she thought, 'Maybe he doesn't want to. Maybe he doesn't really love us.'

(From Words for Today 2001*)*

● Are there connections between this and what we were thinking about *being* and prayer?

● If we are so busy for God that we never find time to *be* with God, can we really love God?

*Love needs time...
not lots
of time,
nor even
regular time,
but quality
time...*

- If we are so busy for God that we never find time to *be* with our friends and family, can we really love God?
- Encourage people to talk about these questions. Do they ring any bells?
- Do people find it more difficult to *be* or to *do?*

ACTION

Listen with all your attention when someone speaks to you or phones. Try, in whatever time is available, to be quiet and let God love you.

- Take back the diaries and watches.

PRAYER

Repeat the prayer used at the beginning.

Blow out the candle.

Study 4 *New Beginnings*

AIM

To celebrate new beginnings and those who make them possible.

Keynote readings
Genesis 12. 1–9
Isaiah 40.27–31; 41.8–13
Luke 5.27–32
Luke 15.11–32

PREPARATION

- *The candle, the stones, the cactus and the cross;*
- *Glue sticks and scissors;*
- *A collection of pictures suggesting despair, sadness and depression from colour supplements, magazines and newspapers;*
- *A large piece of paper or card. Draw a simple flower shape on it, with a stalk. The size depends on the size of your group. The pictures will be cut up and used to fill the petals, like a mosaic.*
- *Prepare the reading from* The Dramatised Bible.

Welcome

Have some music of your choice playing fairly quietly. Before people arrive, put the flower shape in the centre. Place the candle fairly centrally with the stone and cactus. Keep the cross ready for later. Scatter all the pictures around the candle and over the floor. As people arrive,

encourage conversation about last session and about the pictures.

When everyone is there, point out the stone and the cactus and encourage the group to talk about what they represent.

Suggest that, for a minute or two, people sit and look at the pictures. Fade out the music and light the candle.

Prayer
In the silence, think of anyone you may have left at home and of the people in this room. Then say, very slowly and with pauses:

God only wants to
look upon you
with love.
Quiet
Still.
Be.

Let your God
love you.

Follow this with a few moments' silence.

A story
The setting is the Rhondda Valley in South Wales. Ferndale Methodist Church is a lovely building. There is a domed ceiling with stars and carved screens. The mine workings cause the land to subside. The building is condemned. It must be pulled down. Things feel very bleak. The older people say, 'It's so sad but there is nothing that we can do. There is no money and no energy.' A teenager says, 'Oh yes there is.' She does a sponsored parachute jump. People are encouraged and enthused. The congregation worships in the little public library among the bookcases. Now there is vision and enormous energy. A new building grows on the same site. It is simple, attractive and very useful. The Church and the people serve God and their community with new enthusiasm.

● Here is a new beginning.

Read Luke 15.11–32 from *The Dramatised Bible*.

● Here is another new beginning.

It's so sad but there is nothing that we can do

42

Give time for some general talk about the two stories.

● Is it possible to pinpoint a moment in each which made a new beginning possible?

Our own experience

The older people at Ferndale felt at rock bottom. The younger son *was* at rock bottom. Suggest that maybe people in the group have felt something like that. Or maybe they know someone who has felt like that; or a depressed neighbourhood; or a despairing country.

● Ask each person to choose the picture that best represents that feeling.

● In twos, talk about why that particular picture was chosen.

Grow a flower

Move the candle and clear the flower shape.

Provide scissors and glue sticks.

The pictures can be cut into pieces and stuck on the petals of the flower.

Let the group organize how it wants to do this.

When the flower is finished:

● Where shall we put the other pictures?

● Shall we add the cross?

● Do we need the candle?

● Do you want to add anything to the picture?

New beginnings

We have changed sad and bad things into a flower. In silence we think of:

the people who maybe helped us to have a new beginning...

those who have helped people we know... friends, counsellors, therapists...

those who help neighbourhoods and countries in both large and small ways ... politicians, workers for peace and justice, workers for conflict resolution ... kind neighbours all, who encourage and inspire new beginnings.

We have changed sad and bad things into a flower

43

ACTION

Remember these people with thanks and prayer and be aware of ways in which we might help.

PRAYER

As you were in the ebb and flow,
as the beginning becomes the ending,
and the ending a new beginning,
be with us
everpresent God.

(Kate McIlhagga, *from* The Pattern of Our Days,
edited by Kathy Galloway, Wild Goose Publications)

Blow out the candle.

Study 5 *Knowing What Lies Ahead*

Keynote readings
Isaiah 50.4–11
Luke 19.28–40
Luke 19.41–44
John 12.1–8

AIM

To consider how we balance looking ahead with living fully today.

PREPARATION

- *The candle;*
- *The stones;*
- *The picture;*
- *The flower picture;*
- *Notebooks and pencils;*
- *Music: a Requiem by Fauré or Mozart, or you could use the beginning of* The Messiah.

Welcome

As people arrive, ask if they would like to move the objects around. When everyone has arrived, encourage conversation about the flower and anything from the previous weeks. If anyone has moved things around, ask if he or she could explain why. Light the candle.

Prayer

Have a few moments of silence, followed by the prayer used at the end of last session.

To plan or not to plan?

Write the answers down. Do not speak!

- Has anyone got anything planned for one day next week? Not an appointment with the doctor – plans for a day out, the theatre, something pleasant.
- Similar plans for six weeks ahead?
- A year ahead? Two years?
- Maybe people would like to share their plans with their neighbours for a minute or two.

As a group

Suggest that some of us may feel uneasy if we do not have our lives fairly well planned.

- Do some of us find it difficult to think further ahead than next week?
- How do we feel when others like things to be more or less planned than we do?

Have a short conversation.

Comment that we know what lies ahead in Jesus' story, but we do not know what lies ahead in our own story.

Read Luke 19.41–44 together.

- What aspects of our national life would make prophets angry or cause Jesus to weep today?
- Where do you foresee disaster? How can we plan ahead to prevent it from happening?
- Where are there signs of hope?

The story of Etty Hillesum (1914–1943)

Etty was a young Jewish woman living in Amsterdam during the Nazi occupation. For the last two years of her life she kept a meticulous diary. She knew that she would be going to one of the concentration camps in a short while. She expected to die. She wrote,

'God is not accountable to us, but we are to him. I know what may lie in wait for us... And yet I find life beautiful and meaningful.

'I know that a new and kinder day will come. I would so much like to live on, if only to express all the love I carry within me. And there is only one way of preparing the new age, by living it even now in our hearts.'

... there is only one way of preparing the new age, by living it even now in our hearts
Etty Hillesum

Etty Hillesum died in Auschwitz on 30 November 1943. She was 29.

(From An Interrupted Life: The Diaries of Etty Hillesum, 1941–1943, *New York: Pantheon, 1983)*

Read Etty Hillesum's words again.

Listen to as much of the music as feels appropriate.

Suggest that maybe Etty prepared for the future by living fully in the present, and have a short conversation if this feels appropriate.

● Does anyone want to change the objects around, or change the flower picture, or add anything?

ACTION

Speak up for the peace and justice Jesus wants. Notice what is loving and hopeful.

PRAYER

> *O God, our creator,*
> *Your kindness has brought us the gift of a new day.*
> *Help us to leave yesterday,*
> *And not to covet tomorrow,*
> *But to accept the uniqueness of today.*

Blow out the candle.

Study 6 *Who Cares?*

Keynote readings
Psalm 118.1–2, 8–29
Luke 22.14–30
Luke 23.26–49
John 19.38–42

AIM

To consider how we face suffering and pain as individuals and together in our family and community.

PREPARATION

● *The candle;*
● *The stones;*
● *The cross;*
● *The flower picture;*
● *A basket of stones (a few more than one per person) and one night light for each;*
● *Tapers.*

Welcome

When people arrive, have the music playing that you used last session. Have everything used in the previous sessions in a pile at the edge of the circle. Keep the stones and the night lights separate. Ask people as they arrive to put things out as they wish. Some may want to add watches and diaries. Encourage conversation about all this and about the last session. When everyone has settled, fade out the music and light the candle.

Sit quietly thinking of the other people in the room.

Remind people of Etty Hillesum. She wrote, 'I know what may lie in wait for us... And yet I find life beautiful and meaningful.'

Suggest that maybe for us it is difficult to accept pain and suffering in the way Etty did ... the pain and suffering that touches us: news of earthquakes or ethnic cleansing, famine and flood, rail and air disasters.

Suggest that people might like to talk with neighbours about their own reactions to pain and suffering in their lives and in the world.

Pass round the basket of stones. Explain that each stone represents a painful time when someone has said: 'Is there a God? Does God care? Who cares?'   Ask everyone to take a stone each and hold it.

I know what may lie in wait for us ... and yet I find life beautiful and meaningful
Etty Hillesum

Prayer

God loves you with
an enormous love.
God only wants to
look upon you
with love.
Quiet
still
Be.

Let your God –
Love you.

Follow this with a few moments' silence.

Suggest that people might add their stones to the arrangement on the floor. Make a cairn or a circle.

A story from Rajah Jacob

My wife and I fled from our home in Colombo, Sri Lanka, as a menacing crowd came towards it on 25 July 1983, and after two hours' refuge in a kind neighbour's kitchen, we came out and saw our house, with all our possessions, burnt to the ground. We spent a month in a refugee camp where we met hundreds more who had even worse experiences. But the beauty of it was that, as the sun went down and the shadows lengthened, all the Christians went into the church in the centre of the compound, to affirm the presence of God, to sing and to praise.

(*From* Words for Today 2001)

Allow as much time as possible for general conversation.

● Are there connections between the stones and the story?

Great numbers of people followed, among them many women...
Luke 23.27, REB

Read aloud Luke 23.26–49: a story of suffering love.

Suggest that people close their eyes and listen.

Read as dramatically as possible.

Follow this with silence.

● How does that passage make you feel?

Invite comments and queries.

In verse 45 (Revised English Bible), we read 'the sun's light failed' and 'the curtain of the temple was torn in two'. Suffering continues in the world and in our lives. Good Friday reminds us that God is there on the cross suffering with us.

● Do we always realize it in our lives?

Invite comments, queries and conversation.

Lights

People might like to take a taper and, from the central candle, light a night light and place it beside their stone.

ACTION

Think of a particular need in your church or community. How can we express the sacrificial love of Christ in a practical way?

Study 7 *Emptiness and Triumph*

AIM

To consider the way we use our power over others.

PREPARATION

- *The candle and all the things you have collected over the weeks.*
- *If you are going to use role play, give two people the scenarios beforehand and suggest that they change the sex of the characters to suit themselves.*
- The Christ we Share *study pack (Methodist Publishing House) or postcards of crucifixion pictures.*
- *Your 'teachings of Jesus' sheet.*

Welcome

Put the candle and all the objects in a pile somewhere out of the circle. As people arrive, ask them to arrange the space or decide to leave it empty. Encourage discussion about what is done.

When everyone has arrived sit quietly...

Prayer

*God loves you with
an enormous love.
God only wants to
look upon you
with love.
Quiet
still
Be.*

*Let your God
Love you.*

Follow this with a few moments' silence.

Keynote readings
Luke 24.1–12
John 20.1–18
John 20.19–23
John 20.24–31

*Let your God
Love you*

Suggest that maybe not everyone is happy about how the room is arranged. Encourage short conversation in twos about this ... then have a short general talk about how the decision was made.

Role play or story

● Doris, aged 80, is told that Barbara, her caring daughter, is planning a weekend break away. Doris gets upset and comes up with reasons why she could not manage. What might she say?

● Ron the church organist lets it be known that he will resign if Janet is asked to play the piano for two or three modern songs in all-age worship. How might Janet feel?

● A really flourishing church would not be as it is without Alan. At the Church Council/PCC he has been known to walk out if the minister does not do things his way. How do the rest of the members feel?

Draw attention to the power in these stories.

Place pictures from the pack on the floor or pass smaller pictures round. Comment that they could be called 'powerful pictures' ... but is it the same kind of power?

Explain what has happened in the previous verses then **read aloud, slowly and clearly, John 20.19–23.**

Suggest that people might look at the pictures and listen.

● How does that story leave people feeling?

Read verses 21 and 22.

● Are there any signs of Jesus using power to get the disciples to do what he wants?

Have some general conversation.

Listen to what Henri Nouwen says:

In and through Jesus we come to know God as a powerless God, who becomes dependent on us. But it is precisely in this powerlessness that God's power reveals itself. This is not the power that controls, dictates and commands. It is the power that heals, reconciles and unites. It is the power of the Spirit. When Jesus appeared people wanted to touch him because 'power came out of him' (*Luke 6.19*).

In and through Jesus we come to know God as a powerless God
Henri Nouwen

It is this power of the divine Spirit that Jesus wants to give us. The Spirit indeed empowers us and allows us to be healing presences. When we are filled with the Spirit, we can not be other than healers.

(from Bread for the Journey, *Darton, Longman and Todd*)

Produce the 'teachings of Jesus' sheet.

● What are the differences between the story of the Church and its use of power ... and the teaching of Jesus?

Talk about this.

ACTION

Continue to think about this question. Consider the ways in which you may use power over others.

PRAYER

O Lord, you give the victory to the weak!

We give it to the strong and talented,

but you give it to the weak.

Amen

Study 8 *The Well of Deepest Joy*

AIM

To remember the God of life and the times we overlook the joy of creation.

PREPARATION

● *Have the collection of items from other weeks available.*
● *A notebook.*
● *An interesting loaf to share.*
● *A chalice.*
● *A jug of wine or grape juice.*
● *Music: Haydn,* The Creation.

Welcome

Have the music playing. Ask people as they arrive to arrange the room as they wish. When everyone has come and settled, fade the music. Light the candle if people want to. Place the bread and wine in the centre of the circle. The group may now want to rearrange the space.

Keynote readings
Luke 24.13–35
John 21.1–14
John 21.15–19
Philippians 1.12–26
Revelation 1.4–8

A God of life and joy?

Hannah is 90. She often mentions that when she was a girl she was not allowed to sew, knit, or play outside on Sunday.

Janet is 60. She still remembers how unkind the chapel members were when her younger sister was pregnant before she married.

Mary is 40 and says she has just finally decided she can wear long earrings to church.

- Has the group got stories like these to share?
- What ideas about God or Jesus would these experiences have suggested at the time?

Read Luke 24.13–35.

- What feelings does this story arouse in you?
- In what ways might we express our joy in the Resurrection?

Personal Reflection

- Recall some time when you believed wholeheartedly 'God is here!'
- Recall the incident surrounding the experience.
- Recall the feelings that were present to you – name them to yourself.
- Why did you feel God was present at that moment?

Pray for the grace to keep in touch with this experience of God. Remember the feelings that surfaced. Write the experience down for yourself.

A cup of blessings

Introduce this activity as you go along:

Take the chalice in one hand and the jug in the other. Pour a little wine in the chalice as you say: 'I thank God for... (name one thing, e.g. a new grandchild or an item of world news or something special that happened in the group).

Pass the jug and chalice to the next person, who says, 'I thank God for...', and so on round the group. Place the chalice and jug in the centre.

Take the bread. Break a good piece and give it to your neighbour with appropriate comment, e.g. 'This is for you

And they knew him in the breaking of bread

Mary... you always make us laugh.' Mary serves her neighbour in the same way, and so on. Eat together.

Pass the chalice: 'God loves you, Mary' and so on round the group.

Dance

In a circle, feet together, moving to the left:

1. Step left foot to the left.
2. Cross right foot behind left foot.
3. Step left foot to the left.
4. Kick with the right foot.
5. Step right foot to the right.
6. Kick with the left foot.

(Thanks to Stella Bristow)

ACTION

Take time to relish the pleasure of life and to rest in God who is our refuge.

PRAYER

Joyful risen Lord,
From the empty tomb you came and declared the end of death.
Thank you for this day of life,
For creation in its wild variety,
For relationships with their complex beauty and satisfaction,
For suffering that can never touch the well of deepest joy,
For now, this moment in our day
When you keep us safe
And become our refuge.

NOTES BY
STEPHEN DAWES

NEW ROADS AHEAD

Study 1 *Change of Direction*

Keynote readings
Acts 9.1–31
Acts 10.1–48

AIM
To reflect on the changes of direction experienced by Paul and Peter and their effects on those around them.

Where are we in the story in Acts?
In the power of the Holy Spirit the new Jewish sect which taught that Jesus is Lord and Messiah has spread out from Jerusalem and begun to encounter the Gentile world. The parent faith is, however, increasingly hostile. Saul, a zealous Pharisee, is actively campaigning against the new movement.

Way in
Arrange for one member of the group to read the following Bible passages, which tell of well-known 'disclosure moments', pausing for two minutes of silent reflection between each one and after the last one:

*'Whom shall
I send? Who
will go for us?'*
Isaiah 6.8, REB

- Exodus 3.1–17;
- Isaiah 6.1–8;
- 1 Samuel 3.1–18;
- Matthew 3.1–17;
- Luke 9.18–36.

Two groups
These five stories tell of momentous moments in the lives of some key Bible characters. Such heady experiences and radical changes of direction are not common, however, in the Bible narratives as a whole. Nor are they repeated very often in the life of any one individual. The two readings in Acts show us two more such moments.

- Divide into two groups: one group to read Acts 9.1–31 and the other to read Acts 10.1–48.

- Write down the main features of the old direction of the key character's life, then those of the new direction, and finally what it was that brought about the change.
- Identify the others caught up in that change and note its effects on them.
- Note in passing any links with the five readings.

Come together

After someone from each group has given a précis of each reading, share your observations, discoveries and comments:

- Invite any members of the group who wish to do so to share their 'disclosure moments' and the effects these had on their lives.
- Can anyone give a recent example of churches or church groups changing direction as a result of such a 'disclosure moment?'

ACTION

Does your church need to hear any of the 'disclosure moments' you have shared in the group? If so, how could this be done?

PRAYER

Bring your session to a close with a time of silent prayer in which each member is invited to reflect on the direction their own life has taken and is taking. End by saying the Grace together.

Study 2 *Crossing New Boundaries*

AIM

To gasp in astonishment at how the early Christians crossed their first boundary, and to look at one particular boundary which must be crossed soon.

Where are we in the story in Acts?

Saul the Persecutor has been converted and become Saul the Preacher. Peter, the leader of the new movement, has learned from an encounter with the Gentile Cornelius in

...The place where you are standing is holy ground
Exodus 4.5

Keynote reading
Acts 11.1–4, 18–26

Caesarea that God has no favourites and that the new faith is for all.

Way in
Ask the group to list as many divisions as you can which put people on either side of a boundary today.

Read Acts 11.1–4 and 18–26.

Identify how many of the boundaries you have listed are found in that ancient division between Jew and Gentile.

The boundary is crossed

God's people cross boundaries

The Bible is full of stories of God's people crossing boundaries and that is the story-line of Acts too. God's people cross boundaries. Even allowing for Luke's graphics, the story of the growth of the Early Church is remarkable. In it we see the transformation of the Christian movement from just another small Jewish sect into a universal new religion. We rightly give Paul the credit for that transformation. Our reading reminds us that Peter deserves a share, as do others we cannot identify. It also illustrates the first and clearest boundary which was crossed in that transformation. For religious Jews there was a fixed and impassable boundary – ethnic, religious and cultural – between themselves and the rest, the *goyim*, the Gentiles. None of our divisions is so deep, nor any of our boundaries so fixed, as those between religious Jews and the rest in the first century AD. Yet our Jewish Christian forebears crossed those borders. Amazing. Amazing grace!

More boundaries are crossed
The history of the Church is full of stories of God's people continuing to cross boundaries. Here you can either brainstorm another list, or give each member of the group a page out of the most recent editions of your Church's newspaper and ask them to find examples there.

Where next?
'We now live in a post-modern world, a global village, in which the Net and the Web are creating a plethora of new on-line communities and a kaleidoscope of cybercultures.'
(Stephen Dawes)

Some members of your group will understand that quotation. Others will not and will need a translation from those who do.

● Is crossing the boundary into this new culture the most urgent task facing today's Church?

PRAYER

Lord, some of us are bewildered in a threatening world; we have glimpsed the future and are confused by what we have seen. Grant us courage, grant us vision, for this boundary we must cross.

Grant us courage, grant us vision

ACTION

Post-modernity and the cyberculture are here to stay, but this is a foreign world to many Christians and churches, who are still tuned in to the 1950s. Why not decide to check out what it all means? Try *Get a grip on the future without losing your hold on the past* (Gerard Kelly, Monarch Books, 1999).

Study 3 *Cross Over and Help us*

AIM

To take an honest look at a most difficult Bible passage and ask if there are any connections at all between the world of the Acts of the Apostles and the world of the Church in the third millennium.

Keynote reading
Acts 16.6–10

Where are we in the story in Acts?
The problems created by Gentiles becoming Christians, as the believers in this new way are now called, have been resolved. The Jerusalem Conference has agreed the rules by which Gentile Christians are to live. (See Acts 15.19–20, 28–29 and 16.4 – though few modern Christians, even those who claim to be 'Bible-believing', observe two of them. Why not?) Saul, now called Paul, is travelling around the eastern Mediterranean area accompanied by Timothy, revisiting and encouraging existing churches and looking to plant new ones.

Way in
Read Acts 16.6–10.

● Who are the 'they' in verse 6?

Look at a map of the eastern Mediterranean area in the first century AD. Identify all the places mentioned. This journey had begun in Jerusalem and Paul had travelled via Antioch, an important centre of the Early Church. Trace his route.

Look at a map of that area now and identify the same places.

● Who are the 'we' in verse 10?

Christianity comes to Europe! But does Acts make much of it?

Warning

If the commentaries on Acts are anything to go by, this passage marks the most momentous boundary crossing of all – Christianity comes to Europe! But does Acts make much of it? Such commentaries are good examples of a Eurocentric or Western understanding of history and of the Church. We see the same thing when this passage is cited, as it so often is, as the beginning of the 'missionary enterprise'.

Tackling the hard question

1. Luke has no difficulty in writing about clear guidance being given directly to Paul and his companions by the Holy Spirit (or the Spirit of Jesus – the two expressions clearly mean the same thing to Luke).
   ● What are we to make of this?
   ● Do we take Luke's language literally? If so, do we conclude that we are missing something today? Or do we decide that the kind of direct experiences which Luke appears to take as normal just no longer happen? Or do we say that Luke's language should not be taken literally?

2. Luke also tells, however, of a vision which requires decision. REB, NJB and NRSV have 'convinced' in verse 10, but GNB has 'we decided' and NIV and RSV have 'concluding' which suggests that Paul and the others had some serious thinking to do about the vision.

A decision had to be made. A decision was made. Its consequences have been incalculable. The Church has to make decisions and take action all the time but occasionally something comes along which proves to be momentous.

● How does either of these ways of looking at things relate to decision-making in the Church today? In today's Church we tend to prefer the word 'discernment' to 'guidance'. Does that make it any easier?

PRAYER

Name and pray for the decision-makers in your Church (local, regional and national) at the moment, the decisions they have to make and the action which will follow.

Study 4 *Do Not be Afraid*

AIM

Keynote reading
Acts 18.1– 21.16

To share the experience of hearing part of the story of Paul's life and mission read aloud.

Where are we in the story in Acts?

Paul and Timothy have crossed into Europe and Paul has seized the opportunity to address the civic leaders of Athens.

Reading and story

Most Bible reading that Christians do or hear is in snippets. Daily Bible reading notes rarely ask you to read more than twenty verses and the Bible passages read in church services are of much the same length. Most of these snippets are lifted out of long and intricate stories, for 'narrative' is by far the most common type of writing in the Bible. Think, for example, of the continuous story which begins at Genesis 1 and ends at 2 Kings 25, which is immediately followed by a shorter version in 1 and 2 Chronicles. Then in the New Testament we have each of the Gospels and the narrative of Acts itself. Recent years have seen a rediscovery of the importance of stories and story, not least in theology and biblical studies. There are no gimmicks and no rules. Just read and listen.

Recent years have seen a rediscovery of the importance of stories and story, not least in theology and biblical studies

PREPARATION

Choose one member of the group beforehand to read this story (Acts 18.1–21.16). Before the story is read, suggest to the group that the reading might be followed by five minutes of silence in which they can reflect on what they have heard or read. Some may prefer to follow the reading in their own Bible, though there is a lot to be said for simply listening.

Read the story. It will take you about twenty minutes to read these four and a half chapters of Acts. Add to that five minutes of quiet reflection time.

In threes
Tell each other what impressions the story made on you, what you felt when the story was being read and what you felt in the silence.

Tell each other if there were any parts of the story which puzzled you or which you could not understand or follow. If the other two can't help, make a note to ask the full group.

All together
Tackle as many of these questions as you can, but don't worry if you don't get past the first:

● What have you learned about Paul from this reading?

● What have you learned about yourself from this reading?

● What have you learned about discipleship and mission from this reading?

● What have you learned about God from this reading?

● What have you learned about each other from this reading?

PRAYER

In a time of silent prayer pray for the 'missionaries' or 'mission-partners' your church supports, and for Christians and congregations in places of crisis or times of difficulty.

ACTION

Suggest to your Worship Committee and your minister that it might be good occasionally to read a story instead of two or three Bible readings and a sermon.

What have you learned about yourself?

Study 5 *The Spirit Leads us on Gently*

AIM

To explore the pictures of the gift of God's Spirit in these six readings.

PREPARATION

Come prepared with a flipchart or a large piece of paper and pens.

A quote to introduce the theme

The New Testament has two different and markedly contrasting pictures of the gift of the Holy Spirit to the Church. There is the gift given in gentle quietness in John 20.19–23 and there is the gift given in noisy dynamism in Acts 2.1–12. Christians invariably prefer one of these passages to the other.

Way in

Divide the group into five and give each group one of the Keynote passages to read (give one group both the Isaiah and Ephesians passages). Ask each group to write up the words or phrases from their reading which refer to the Holy Spirit or describe the work of the Spirit when they have identified them in their passage.

Together

Study the flipchart:

● See if any of the words or pictures have turned up more than once.

● See if any of the words or pictures can be grouped together.

● Discuss what these readings understand the work of the Spirit in the life of the Church and the Christian to be.

● Talk about which images you are most comfortable with and which make you uneasy and why.

Look up

Look through the hymns in the Holy Spirit section of the hymn book(s) used in your church(es). Note those which speak of the Holy Spirit in a context of gentle quietness

Keynote readings
John 14.15–31
John 15.18–27
John 16.1–15
Luke 24.44–53
Isaiah 44.1–8
Ephesians 4.7–16

'I shall pour out my Spirit on your offspring and my blessing on your children'
Isaiah 44.3

Come down, O love Divine, Seek thou this soul of mine

(two certainties will be 'Come down, O Love Divine' and 'Breathe on me, breath of God').

Dictionary note

The Greek word *paraklete*, which is found five times in these verses from John, is used without translation in NJB. It appears as 'Helper' or 'Counsellor' in other modern versions, sometimes with a capital letter, sometimes not. It is a word taken from the language of the law courts where it was used for a defending counsel or attorney.

PRAYER

Select and sing one of the hymns you have found as a prayer.

Study 6 *The Spirit Leads us on Tumultuously*

Keynote readings
Acts 2.1–21
Romans 8

AIM

To explore the pictures of the gift of God's spirit in these two readings.

Way in

Exactly as last time. Come prepared with a flipchart or a large piece of paper and pens. Divide into two groups and allocate one of the key readings to each. Ask each group to write up the words or phrases from their reading which refer to the Holy Spirit or describe the work of the Spirit when they have identified them in their passage.

Together
Study the flipchart:

● See if any of the words or pictures have turned up more than once.

● See if any of the words or pictures can be grouped together.

● Discuss what these readings understand the work of the Spirit in the life of the Church and the Christian to be.

● Talk about which images you are most comfortable with and which make you uneasy and why.

Talk about which images you are most comfortable with and which make you uneasy and why

Two questions

The Bible reading in most mainstream churches at Pentecost will almost invariably be the one from Acts 2. It will be read and preached about as if it is an eyewitness account of what actually took place on that particular Day of Pentecost. Yet for most of the members of those churches, that reading will not relate to their experience. Why, then, do we go on using it? Why, too, do our preachers not tell us that it is not necessarily to be taken as a piece of history?

Three quotes and some more questions

'Of the issues which have divided modern Christians across the world – abortion, divorce, the Church and politics, human sexuality, the ministry of women, the use of the Bible, the Holy Spirit – it is the last which has proved the most creative, the most divisive and the most provocative of them all.'

● Do you agree? If so, why do you think this is?

'The Charismatic Movement, which burst onto the European Church scene in the 1970s, has transformed the Church, bringing new life and vitality, new songs for singing and new ways for worshipping. In it God has filled a countless number of old and new Christians with new energy, new love and new power. Thanks be to God for this outpouring of his love.'

● Do you agree? If so, why do you think this is?

'The twentieth century began with Christendom divided into three parts – Orthodox, Roman Catholic and Protestant. It ended with a newcomer – the Pentecostal – fast outstripping them all.'

● Do you agree? If so, why do you think this is?

ACTION

If your group consists of people like me who are happiest with the John 20 picture of the gift of the Spirit, why not make a decision to talk – over coffee at home or in your group – to one or two members of your local charismatic group or church?

If your group consists of those whose experience is like that of Acts 2, why not make a decision to talk – over

They were all filled with the Holy Spirit...
Acts 2.4

coffee at home or in your group – to one or two members of your local non-charismatic church?

The point of such a conversation would not be to convert, argue or harangue, but to listen; for the New Testament – and the Church – contains both John 20 and Acts 2.

PRAYER

Faithful God, you fulfilled the promise of Easter by sending your Holy Spirit. Keep us in the unity of your Spirit, that every tongue may tell of your glory and every life may live and work to your praise in the power of your Spirit. Amen

Study 7 *Letting Go of the Past*

Keynote reading
Galatians 1–3

AIM

To examine and critique different responses to change and to explore our own.

Some slogans

'Change equals catastrophe'

'Change equals improvement'

'No change – bad: all change – good'

'No change – good: all change – bad'

Background

Galatians is an angry letter. It is abusive and rude. Read 5.12 if you think I'm overstating things. It was written in the heat of violent controversy and it shows. Paul is dictating at the top of his voice. Time and again he starts to make a point and then something triggers a new outburst which means that his original sentence never gets finished. We have actually met this controversy before, in the chapters of Acts we looked at in studies 1 and 2 about **Change of Direction** and **Crossing New Boundaries**. There, however, we were reading what Luke had to say about it years later. In Galatians we are in the thick of what Paul saw as a life or death battle for the very soul of the Church. But so did those he castigates and abuses. Change can evoke deep emotions – anger, resentment, fear – and invite conflict.

Change can evoke deep emotions – anger, resentment, fear – and invite conflict

Warning

'Letting go of the past' is a loaded phrase. It implies that letting go of the past is a good, if not essential, thing to do. It points an accusing finger at those who don't want to do it. But who decides? And how?

Way in

Divide into sixes. Give each person in the six a name: Peter (Cephas) and Barnabas, Paul and Titus, Menahem and Reuben who are friends of James from Jerusalem. **Read Galatians 2.11–14**. Imagine that each pair has just returned to their separate lodgings in Antioch after this incident. Spend five minutes in the pairs recreating the conversation over your bedtime glass of wine. Come together in your six and let each pair spend five minutes telling the other four people what they felt like and what they have said. Then spend five minutes reflecting on the exercise.

Next

Leave the particular situation in Galatians behind now. Do not try to explore further the specific issues involved. If you are interested in doing that, do it at some other time. For now think of them as 'old, unhappy, far-off things and battles long ago'.

Update

Without discussing any of them, identify half a dozen modern issues in the Church (local, national or international) which are fundamentally the same as this one: i.e. arguments about how much of a precious past should be kept or lost.

Share

Share your feelings about these Victorian words from the American poet James Russell Lowell, which we used to sing in the hymn 'Once to every man and nation, comes the moment to decide':

New occasions teach new duties;
Time makes ancient good uncouth;
They must upward still and onward
Who would keep abreast of truth.

Reflect on the hymn 'Lord God, by whom all change is

'Letting go of the past' is a loaded phrase

wrought'. Note how it speaks of both change and changelessness.

PRAYER
Say or sing that hymn.

Study 8 *Two Contrasting Ways*

Keynote reading
Galatians 5.13–26

AIM
To examine our lives, values and attitudes in the light of Galatians 5.22–23 and 5.25.

Background
Almost at the end of a passionate and sometimes vitriolic letter, we read this classic text about Christian values and virtues. It contrasts two opposing ways – the way of the 'Spirit' and the way of the 'flesh' and urges all who 'live by the Spirit' (i.e. every Christian) to 'walk by the Spirit' (verse 25).

'Flesh' is a tricky term

'Flesh' is a tricky term. It is used in the New Testament for humanity in our weakness and frailty, though with increasingly strong overtones of our badness and sinfulness. REB refers here to our 'unspiritual nature', NIV to our 'sinful nature', NJB to 'self-indulgence' while GNB too starkly calls it our 'human nature'. The image of two contrasting 'ways' in which we can chose to 'walk' is an old one in the Bible, having its roots in the wisdom writings of the Old Testament which invite us to walk on the path of wisdom and not that of folly *(see Proverbs 1–4)*. Jesus uses the same old picture in Matthew 7.13–14. The metaphor points out that serious choices are to be made about values and lifestyles.

Way in
First, share what you feel about the phrase 'Back to basics'. Then do the same about the phrase 'Core values'.

The ideal
The 'fruit of the Spirit'. Galatians 5.22–23 is a well-known and straightforward text. Arrange for as many Bible translations as possible to be available and share them out among the group. Give each member of the group nine pieces of card and ask them to write each of the virtues

listed in their version on a separate card. Collect them into nine piles and talk about some of the different translations you have discovered. Then reflect silently on what you see.

The real

In reality our attitudes and values, let alone our actual words and deeds – personally and corporately in the Church – often fall well below the ideal of Galatians 5.22–23. But so did Paul's, for Galatians 5.12 is surely a prime example of a 'work of the flesh'.

● How do we cope with the gap in our lives and our churches between the ideal and the real?

The way forward?

● Is Galatians 5.25 the key?

It begins by pointing out that the new life we have received as Christians is from God, the work of his Spirit. It then goes on to point out what this new life then asks of us. Compare your translations of the second half of the verse, for they vary a little, but RSV is best here.

● What does Paul's appeal to the Galatians in this way mean for you?

I don't know where it comes from, but 'the relevance of the impossible ideal' is a phrase I have treasured for years.

● Is it a helpful one here?

... the relevance of the impossible ideal

ACTION

If need be, go back to basics and change your values and attitudes.

PRAYER

> *Dear Master, in whose life I see*
> *All that I would, but fail to be,*
> *Let Thy clear light for ever shine,*
> *To shame and guide this life of mine.*
>
> *Though what I dream and what I do*
> *In my weak days are always two,*
> *Help me, oppressed by things undone,*
> *O Thou, whose deeds and dreams were one.*

(John Hunter, 1848–1917)

NOTES BY
BILL DENNING

SUFFERING AND A GOD OF LOVE

NOTES FOR THE LEADER

Each week there is:

- an **exercise** to enable participants to identify more readily with the theme.

- a **Gospel story** and **psalm** which can interact and throw light on each other. They are related through 'role-reading' – using imagination to become the person in the story, then reading the psalm in that role not by going round the room, which can be threatening for some, but by all reading, two groups alternating or people reading randomly. Please note that some studies use different readings from those in *Words for Today*, but still relate to the overall theme.

- a different **creative** option: colour, writing, clay and meditation. For the fifth week, the group decides which of the forms to use again. Remember, creativity is not necessarily about skills but about the risks people are prepared to take. Do not judge or joke about anything that anyone makes. Quietness is important to help people to get in touch with themselves.

- the image of a **stile:** a means of getting over a barrier or fence. Use the idea of the stile, with reflection on what has emerged through the creativity, to explore how we 'get over' difficult barriers and move on. A key question to help get the reflection going is something like: 'How did you **feel** when you were working with the pastels, clay…?'

Practical preparation

Art Materials:

For colour – children's pastels and cheap paper;

For modelling – hardboard squares about 20cm x 20cm;

For clay – ask a local school or pottery.

If no real clay is available, consider doing something like collage. Remember, the process matters more than the finished product.

Study 1 'Why Have you Abandoned me?'

AIM

Keynote readings
Luke 8.26–39
Psalm 42

To understand feeling abandoned by God as a normal human experience, and to see how feeling perplexed and angry may be healthy and creative.

Exercise

- Invite the group to recall experiences of being abandoned or pushed away or rejected.

- Ask what they felt at the time, and then what they feel in the present recalling the memory. *Note down those feelings.*

- Encourage people to be willing to acknowledge that they have felt abandoned by God and to name some of the feelings surrounding that experience.

- Invite them to imagine how Jesus might have felt on the cross when he cried out: 'My God, why have you forsaken me?' *Note down the feelings that are expressed.*

Read the story in Luke 8.26–39.

'My God, why have you forsaken me?'

- Invite the group to identify any rejection experiences in the story.

- Invite the group to imagine how the man felt living amongst the tombs, and then how he felt when Jesus sent him back home. *Note the feelings that are suggested.*

- Look back at the list of original 'rejection feelings' expressed by the group and compare them with this second list.

Prepare to read Psalm 42.

- Invite the group members to imagine they are the man and now read Psalm 42 as if it were being read by him. *(See the leader's notes on 'role-reading'.)*

- Select the phrases in the psalm that echo what the man might have felt before the healing and after it.

- Ask when and where group members have felt just like that.

Creativity – *Colour.* Pastels or crayons and paper.

- Invite the group to explore and express anything in the story that has touched them. If they want ideas, suggest

Where is your God?
Psalm 42.3

the loneliness and abandonment of the man before his healing and afterwards when he is sent back home when he wants to follow Jesus. (Do remind them that skill is totally unnecessary and all they need to do is to start and see what happens.)

Reflection
● Ask the group how they felt about using pastels if this is not something they often do; go on to ask what they were feeling and thinking while doing it.

● Encourage people to be honest about some questions they would like to put to God.
● Go to Psalm 42 and ask the group to pick out the questions that are asked in it and to say which is the one that most echoes their own heartfelt questioning.
● If you are using the stile as an image for getting over a barrier and moving on, ask what 'stiles' we have discovered to assist us to 'get over' the problem of struggling with what feels to be the 'absence of God'.

ACTION
Think about the people in your own community who may feel that God is absent and does not answer their prayers. Could this be a hospice or hospital where loved ones are dying? Consider whether there is any practical loving

action that could be undertaken for one person known to the group.

PRAYER

O God who has promised always to be with us:
forgive us when we cannot see your love
or hear you speak in one another.
Open our eyes so that we may perceive you at work
in the compassion of our friends
and open our ears
so that we may feel you call to us in their need.
Through Jesus Christ we pray.
Amen

Open our eyes
so that we may
perceive you
at work

Study 2 *Weep with Those who Weep*

AIM

To explore and understand empathy as active engagement.

Keynote readings
Mark 8.22–26
Psalm 84

Exercise

Part 1

- Ask the group to imagine what it might be like to be blind or partially sighted.

- If there is sufficient space, ask the group to form pairs: one agrees to be 'blind' – and no cheating is allowed! The seeing partner then takes the 'blind one' for a short walk, inviting them to use other senses like touch and smell. After five minutes, change roles.

- Get some feedback from the group on how the exercise went. How did it feel to be visually impaired and to have someone to guide, protect and open up alternative possibilities for you?

Part 2

- Invite the group privately to recall an experience when they were deeply hurt.

- Ask what the feelings were. *Note them down.*

- Enquire whether they were alone in all this or whether others were there with them, sharing their experience by 'guiding, protecting and opening up possibilities'.

Hearts set ... on the pilgrim ways
Psalm 84.5

Read Mark 8.22–26.

● Draw attention to the story where some people 'brought' a blind man to Jesus and 'begged' him to 'touch' him.

● Explore what it would be like to be really blind.

● Ask people if there were others who felt so strongly for them, that they felt carried by them to a healing place. Three focal points are important – they 'brought' him where he could not go himself and they 'begged' Jesus to 'touch 'him.

Introduce and role-read Psalm 84.

Introduce the psalm by suggesting that God's 'dwelling place' is the experience of closeness and security that is a true home. Stress the corporate 'they' who travel together. Link this with the group of people bringing the blind man and sharing his journey.

● Ask people to say which phrase or verse meant most to them as they imagined themselves to be the blind man.

Creativity – *Creative Writing.*

Suggest that the group members write their own psalm as if they were the healed man who is deeply grateful for what has happened and how it came about. There could be two ways of doing this writing:

● **Individually,** with the possibility of sharing afterwards – though there should be no pressure to do this.

● **As a group** – prepare a psalm with short, simply worded contributions.

It could be done in three stages:

● **Tell** God what is happening and what you feel.

● **Ask** God for what you feel you now need in the changed present and unknown future.

● **Thank** God for all that has happened and will happen.

Reflection

● Explore what happened in the dark places to get people over the stile and enable them to move on.

*Forgive us
when we do not
see the needs
of others*

ACTION

Think about a person or group of people locally who experience severe limitation and cannot do certain things. How can we take them where they cannot go themselves – moving beyond sympathy to positive creative help?

PRAYER

*God most faithful and loving,
who calls us to bring one another
into your healing presence
by our words and actions:
forgive us when we do not see the needs of others
and are unaware of our own brokenness.
Enable us by your Spirit
to take our sisters and brothers
to the place where they are touched by caring love
and warmed by compassionate understanding.
Through Jesus Christ we pray. Amen.*

Study 3 *God of Healing*

AIM

To explore how God's love meets the suffering of the excluded by touching them through us.

Keynote readings
Luke 5.12–16
Psalm 30

Leader's introduction

The leper was deemed to be unclean, and could not touch or be touched. In addition the illness would have been seen as a punishment by God for wrong-doing. The leper was excluded. We are shocked by these taboos but there are just as many destructive attitudes today. Healing that can be experienced as the work of God in society is more than curing a persistent illness. It involves the whole person and society itself, where changed attitudes and values and moves towards inclusiveness and acceptance are signs of God's renewing presence.

Exercise

● Invite group members to recall a time when they were excluded from a group or perhaps made to feel unclean and unwelcome, and where they were quite alone in that experience. How did it feel?

Read the story in Luke 5.12–16.

● Ask the group what they noticed most of all in the story in order to find out what has touched them. The responses will reflect the previous exercise.

● Ask the group to imagine what the man must have felt:
○ over the time of his illness with its exclusion from others and his physical condition;
○ when he knew that Jesus was around and he, the untouchable, dared to appeal to the good will of Jesus: 'If you want to, you can cure me.'
○ when Jesus exclaimed: 'Of course I want to...' and touched him and he was cured.

Prepare to read Psalm 30.

As a group, role-read the psalm, and invite people to pick out phrases the man might have said with deep feeling.

Creativity – *Clay* (or collage if clay is not available).

Remind the group of the desirability of working in silence, and give each person a lump of clay to hold in their hands. They should close their eyes, and let their hands shape the clay without thinking about it.

Reflection and the 'stile'

Explore where the quiet creativity and the clay have taken people in their thoughts and feelings.

The barrier that the man had to face was that he should not come near to Jesus and it took immense courage and risk to do so. Reflect on the meaning of this story today.

- Who are the excluded ones in our society and where does healing happen for them?
- Ask the group to look at their own inner feelings of exclusion. Where is healing happening in their lives? Who is the presence of Christ the healer for them?

ACTION

Explore the possibility of identifying marginalized people in the church or in the neighbourhood, and think about how those people could experience the healing touch of Jesus.

PRAYER

*Loving gracious God, whose presence
is seen and felt through those whose lives meet ours:
forgive us when we exclude our sisters and brothers
whose ways we do not understand
or whose lifestyle we resent.
Open our hearts with the costly compassion of Jesus
that we might touch with healing love
and in that touch
may ourselves become more whole.
Through Jesus Christ we pray. Amen*

Study 4 *The Healing Church*

AIM

To explore experiences of the church community as a place of wholeness.

Keynote readings
Luke 17.11–19
Psalm 87

Way in

The community of love that the Church should be is both fragile and human and yet it is, at its best, a place of healing where loving care and understanding are the presence of Christ to those who are suffering. The God of love is in the suffering and heals through the community of love that can be a true 'home'.

Wholeness is not the same as cure

Wholeness is not the same as cure. The healing community that the church can be is not a place for instant cures but a resource centre for those who want to become whole.

Exercise

● Recall someone suffering through illness, need or bereavement.

● How did the Church relate to that person?

● What is meant by 'the Church' that did or did not relate to that suffering?

Read Luke 17.11–19.

Reflect with the group on one or all of the following issues:

● Jesus often touches the sick, but he does not in this instance and they keep their distance. How does that feel to us?

● He sends them to the synagogue to see the priests – this suggests a religious ritual. Is there a place for healing rituals today? What might these be?

● Only one returns to give thanks and he, the Samaritan, the most excluded of all, hears the words of Jesus: 'your faith has saved you' (JB). This surely is moving beyond cure to wholeness.

● How important is gratitude in the healing process?

Prepare to read Psalm 87.

The Jerusalem Bible concludes the psalm with the words: 'All find their home in you'.

Role-read the psalm, perhaps choosing to see the 'city of God' as an image of the Church community – the people of God, where all may find their true home. Role-read it as the healed Samaritan and talk about how he would feel, having found himself accepted by Jesus and 'at home' with him.

Creativity – *Meditation*

There is no right or wrong way to imagine. Tell the group that you will simply make suggestions – they will then fill in the details. There will be silent spaces and it will end with more silence.

- Invite the group to become comfortable and still and then ask them to imagine their ideal, beautiful home where they would most like to live. Give them plenty of time to think quietly, perhaps suggesting they explore what they can see, hear and smell. Allow time for the imagination to wander.

- Next, invite them to go to the still place or space in this home where they would most like to be. Again the senses are important.

- Now suggest that Jesus comes to this room. What do you want to ask of him? What does he say and do to you?

- Invite the group silently to give thanks, as the Samaritan did, and leave another minute of total quiet before moving on to the next stage.

Reflection

Enquire gently how the group felt about the meditation. Some may have found it difficult.

In the light of the Bible study, ask what 'stiles' have helped them get over difficulties in seeing the local congregation as a healing community.

The source of all good is in you
Psalm 87.7

ACTION

As a group, write a short prayer of thanksgiving for the Church as a place of healing.

PRAYER

O loving God in whom all may find their true home:
forgive the Church when it chooses not to include those
who are unacceptable
and forgive us when we receive so much with little
gratitude.
We give you thanks for the community of love that
heals us
and ask you to show us by your Spirit
how to find within it
true wholeness for our bodies and our souls
and enable us to be the healing presence of Christ
to one another.
In his name we pray. Amen

We give you thanks for the community of love that heals us

Study 5 *Trial and Trust*

Keynote readings
Luke 8.22–25
Psalm 46

AIM

To find the still place when storm and chaos surround us.

Leader's notes

It is easy to be superficial and make people feel guilty if they do not easily find a still centre. This therefore is not about a quick-fix approach, but about developing a lifestyle that builds into it a routine of quiet stillness that is a joy when life is good and becomes a resource when life is harsh.

Exercise

Have a candle not yet lit, surrounded by pieces of jagged broken glass.

Invite the group to suggest experiences that are, like the broken glass, sharp and painful and create upheaval and chaos. The group might also wish to write on pieces of paper some of the feelings that go with this, and to add those pieces to the glass.

Read Luke 8.22–25.

Invite the group to think of groups of people or whole communities who may feel themselves to be in a boat that is sinking with huge frightening waves beating down on them.

- Ask what those people would feel.
- Imagine and note what their questions might be.
- Explore what might provide a calming stillness at the centre of the storm where they might feel some peace even if the 'waves' of destructive experiences are crashing round them.

Prepare to read Psalm 46.
Role-read the psalm as if the group were the disciples and then invite them to select the verses or phrases that most reflect their own experience.

- Talk about the obstacles that have to be overcome in trying, each day, to build into our lives times of stillness and quiet that can be a point of calm at the heart of the storm.

Creativity
Use whatever medium the group has chosen for this week: writing, colour, clay or meditation.

Reflection
Light the candle and reflect on how the flame of the candle is a still centre surrounded by brokenness; note how the flame lights up the glass pieces and transforms them.

Most of us get tired of Christians who offer neat solutions to complex problems or who have an answer for everything. Without falling into that trap, what 'stiles' have helped us come to terms with appalling tragedy and have enabled us, even in the worst of storms, to find a still and peaceful centre?

There is a river whose streams bring joy
Psalm 46.4

ACTION

Could the members of the group consider committing themselves, for one week, to beginning and ending each day with quiet stillness and silently repeating several times, 'Be still and know that I am God'?

PRAYER

O God who calls us to be still
when the familiar mountains are breaking up
and falling into the sea
and chaos surrounds us on every side:
forgive us that we forget your presence so easily
and become fearful and anxious.
Show us that you stay by our side
when we enter the darkness
and that you share our deepest pain
through those in whom we see the face of Christ.
Through him we pray. Amen

GOD OF LOVE AND ANGER
(BOOK OF HOSEA)

Study 1 *Mixed Messages*

AIM

To explore some of the conflicting messages found in Hosea.

Keynote reading
Hosea 1.1–11

PREPARATION

Cut out two large circles of thin card, about 30cm (12") in diameter. On one draw a face with a smile and on the other draw a face with a frown.

To think about

Place the two 'faces' where the whole group can see them.

Invite group members to name as many messages as they can think of which are communicated through a smile. Write each response on a small piece of paper and place it beside the face with a smile.

Do the same with the cut-out face with a frown.

To puzzle over
Read Hosea 1.1–11.

The underlying message of Hosea is to communicate God's continuing love for the people even though they repeatedly choose to behave in ways which reject God.

There are difficulties with the text for us today when we read it from our context. Hosea's use of his own family in order to get a message across may have had underlying good intentions but, as people, they ended up carrying the main burden of his prophecy. The strength of the destructive messages which are given about women and children is seen quite differently today from the way it might have been in Hosea's day. Gomer is 'used' as a central character in this real-life 'role-play'. She is forgotten as a person in her own right and is cast as the

There are difficulties with the text for us today when we read it from our context

shameful one, representing the people of Israel. Two of the children from Hosea and Gomer's marriage – Loruhamah (which means 'not pitied') and Loammi (which means 'not my people') – are condemned to carry names of utter rejection. Hosea, by implication and in sharp contrast, casts or places himself as the 'god character' – the one who demonstrates unfailing love.

As Rabbi Professor Jonathan Magonet writes in *Words for Today*:

Sometimes we have to read against the grain of a Biblical text

> 'Sometimes we have to read against the grain of a Biblical text and not simply accept it or its presuppositions, at face value.'

To discuss

● In your view, what would you name as the conflicting messages found in Hosea?

● In what ways do you think Hosea's message reinforces our understanding of God?

● In what ways does his message challenge our understanding of God?

To reflect and pray

This litany focuses on the names of the five named people in Hosea's prophecy. Between each section, group members can be invited to name those who come to mind as a result of the words of the litany. This may include names of known people. On the other hand, it may be a group of people or an organization which comes to mind. Equally, it may be that a time of silence is observed instead.

Light a candle beside the two 'faces' used at the start of the session.

We remember before God those who come to mind:

In the name of Hosea...
a man who knew that actions speak louder than words;
a prophetic voice amongst people reluctant to hear.

We remember those whose actions speak to us of love even when we are reluctant to hear.

(Pause)

In the name of Gomer...

a woman cast as one who represents all that is wrong with the people;

a mother, rejected along with her children, as unloved.

We remember those who are cast in an unfavourable light and whom we reject without taking the time to understand them.

(Pause)

In the name of Jezreel...

the first-born of a relationship founded on a covenant rather than passion;

the first-fruits of the seeds of God's hope.

We remember those who wonder why they are alive and with whom we are invited to journey.

(Pause)

In the name of Loruhamah...

the daughter who was not pitied;

the girl whose name breathes the sounds of desolation.

We remember those whose times of sorrow are not shared with others and whose cries we prefer not to hear.

(Pause)

In the name of Loammi...

the second son whose origins meant that reconciliation with his father could never be complete;

the last in the line of a litany for the children of God.

We remember those who long for acceptance and inclusion and whose needs we cannot afford to ignore.

(Pause)

God says, 'It is I who answer and look after you.
I am like an evergreen cypress:
your faithfulness comes from me.'

(Hosea 14.8, NRSV)

'I am like an evergreen cypress: your faithfulness comes from me'
Hosea 14.8, NRSV

Study 2 *The Torment of Love*

Keynote reading
Hosea 11.1–11

AIM

To explore Hosea's picture of God as both powerful and impotent as a result of love.

PREPARATION

Slips of paper about 5cm x 10cm (2" x 4") need to be prepared. There should be enough so that each group member could use three or four.

Way in

Distribute the slips of paper to members of the group.

Invite each member to write one word or phrase which they associate with love on a slip of paper.

Then ask the group members to tear each slip in half. All the torn pieces are then placed in a basket or bowl and placed to one side until the end of the discussion.

To puzzle over
Read Hosea 11.1–11.

Hosea speaks of God as one in torment. The long-cherished relationship with the people is in serious jeopardy. Reassurances offered and promises given in the past now appear to have lost all hold. Other influences have offered more attractive options and all that once seemed so sure and steady, indeed covenanted, is now of least interest to the people. God as the one betrayed looks with love, tormented by two equally strong urges. On the one hand, anger takes its hold and the desire to bring devastation on the people in order to teach them a lesson increases in its strength. Surely God, as the all-powerful creator of all things, can show the people how wrong they are and make them return to their first love.

Love alone will bring the people to their senses

On the other hand, anger, violence and destruction do not teach love – they only strengthen isolation and fear. Love alone will bring the people to their senses. Memories of past tendernesses, careful nurture and close companionship are what will help them to return to where they need to be.

Such is the nature of the torment. With every passing moment the risk is that the people will go further and further away, and love as God intends it to be will be forgotten. But, if love is to be expressed truly, it has to be because it is not forced upon them. There will be a time when the consistency of God's love will once again dawn upon the people's consciousness and the strong memories from the past will help them to recover. When this happens, God will receive them again with the same love which had always been there.

To discuss

- What kinds of situations are there in life when love is more powerfully expressed by letting go than by holding on?
- Why do you think Hosea portrays God as one in torment?
- To what extent should love and anger be viewed as opposites?

To what extent should love and anger be viewed as opposites?

To reflect and pray

Empty out the pieces of paper which were placed in a basket/bowl at the beginning of the session onto a large sheet of paper on the floor or table (whichever is more visible or suitable for the group). Each piece should be turned with the writing facing up. Do not try to piece the original pieces back together, but leave them scattered in a random fashion.

Spend a few moments reflecting on the visual symbolism of these pieces of paper.

Invite different group members to read each of the following lines:

- Here are the broken remnants of love.
- We both made them and tore them apart.
- The pieces are all here, should we choose to put them together.
- Where we ripped them there will always be a tear.
- All we would need to put them together again is time and patience.

(Pause)

When you were a child, I loved you.
It was I who taught you to walk.

I took you up in my arms, but you did not know that I healed you.
I led you with cords of human kindness, with bands of love.
I bend down to you and feed you.
I will not execute my fierce anger.
I will not destroy you,
For I am God and no mortal
I will not come in wrath.
(Adapted from Hosea 11.1, 3–4, 9)

The God of peace, hope and love is with us now and for evermore. Amen

NOTES BY
JAN SUTCH PICKARD

THE POWER OF DREAMING

Study 1 *In Your Dreams*

AIM

To practise listening to each other and to our imaginations.

PREPARATION

Sheets of drawing paper and pens/pencils will be needed, as well as text references written out on separate cards (see below).

Method

● When the group has gathered, take time to listen to one another. Ask, 'How are you?'. Listen to the answers, observing two disciplines: that each speaker is reasonably brief (say two minutes); and that no one interrupts or turns the sharing into a discussion. If studying on your own, write down single words to sum up things that have been good, bad, hard or hopeful in the last week.

● Ask, 'In the last week have you had any memorable dreams? What did you make of them?' Again, listen. Observe a short silence. Now members of the group may comment on anything said by others.

● Together compile a list of names of folk in the Old and New Testaments who have had significant dreams.

● Play *Pictionary!* Have the references for the *Keynote Readings* written out on separate cards. An individual or small group should each take one and read the passage quietly. Then, gathered in the larger group, take turns to draw and guess the dreamer and the dream. Have fun!

Comment

Those dreams were sometimes about personal circumstances but the larger picture is the story of a people encountering God. So Genesis 32.22–32 is about an experience as private as a dream, but with a physical

Keynote readings
Genesis 32.22–32
Genesis 37.1–11
Genesis 40.1–23
Genesis 41.14–32

'How are you?'

...wrestling with a difficult blessing

dimension that leaves its mark on the dreamer – Jacob wrestling with a difficult blessing.

Ask

● Have there been times in your life when a dream has said something important to you?

● Jacob also saw a ladder between earth and heaven, with angels. What, for you, would be a picture of hope?

Prayer

Mysterious God,
we wrestle for a meaning in our lives;
we are both scarred and blessed
by our experience.
Help us to understand
how in the imagery of dreams –
fearful, delightful, personal, hopeful –
we may come face to face with you.

Sing together 'Be Thou My Vision'.

ACTION

Keep pen and paper by your bed and write down any dreams you remember on waking, over the next week.

Study 2 *Signs of the Times*

Keynote readings
Daniel 2.1–47
Luke 4.16–30

AIM

To reflect, through Old Testament and New Testament stories, how we might discern and respond to 'signs of the times' today.

PREPARATION

● *If possible, photocopy Daniel 2.1–47 and mark up different parts for dramatized reading (see below). Or make sure that all the group have the same version of the Bible.*

● *Have daily papers available.*

Welcome

Welcome the group and spend a short time sharing any remembered dreams from the past week. Don't spend too much time trying to interpret them for one another!

Read together **Daniel 2.1–47**, dramatizing it by taking the following parts:

● Narrator;
● Nebuchadnezzar;
● Chaldeans/magicians etc. (several voices together);
● Daniel;
● Arioch.

Either read Kathy Galloway's comments on this story from IBRA's *Words for Today 2001* (19–21 August) or together share what you know about the background to this story, and what you imagine to be the viewpoints and dilemmas of the different characters, from reading it.

Search the newspapers for one or more stories which are about a crisis or challenging situation in our own times, local, national or international. Share what you have found with each other and reflect on these.

Read **Luke 4.16–30**. Discuss:

● Why was Jesus' message so disturbing to his hearers? How can this prophecy (Isaiah 61.1–6) be read as relevant to our world today?

● When we look at signs of the times and shared dreams, what are some of the criteria we use for discernment?

● Where do we find discernment most difficult?

PRAYER

Blessed be God for ever,
who lives in time and eternity;
Blessed be God who loves justice and mercy
and pays heed to each body and soul;
Blessed be God, whose kingdom is at hand;
Blessed be God, who heals and forgives those who fall;
Blessed be God, who comes to save the oppressed
and lifts the poor from the doors of despair;
Blessed be God, in whom is our hope and our trust
who puts songs in the hearts of people.
(Kathy Galloway, based on Daniel 2.20b–22)

Blessed be God,
who puts
songs in
the hearts
of people

ACTION

Remind yourself of a long-cherished dream for your own life, work, community or church, and make notes, or discuss with others how it might be made to work.

Study 3 *Dreams to Share*

Where concrete seemed to have covered every growing thing, there were folk who chose to make a garden

AIM

Sharing an experience of a broken dream, to understand our need for God's grace – and the restoring power of God's love.

Begin by asking whether anyone has a dream from the past week that they want (or need) to share. If someone does, let them tell it briefly. But don't force it!

A story

In the heart of the city, there were dreamers. Where concrete seemed to have covered every growing thing, there were folk who chose to make a garden. They got permission from the Council to take over a space where tenements had been demolished and no new building was planned for some time.

Led by a retired civil servant who loved the countryside although he had always lived in the city, a great mixture of folk became involved: elderly residents with no gardens of their own; unemployed young people; a bus driver who grew up on a Caribbean island smallholding; local primary school children; conservation volunteers. They cleared rubble, discovered pockets of topsoil, raised money to buy several trees, fenced off the dangerous canal – but encouraged its wildlife – laid paths and made seats and places for children to play, and begged cuttings and grass-seed. They created a wildflower meadow. The garden took shape; it belonged to everyone.

By the end of that first summer in which many folk had worked and played in the garden, it was possible to see how good it could be – something for everyone to enjoy.

In the dark and rainy autumn not many folk visited the garden. Then one day the man who had the dream in the first place stopped at the gate and saw it had been vandalized: the young trees broken off, rubbish dumped in the middle, seats smashed and dragged across grass and flower-beds to be thrown into the canal, and graffiti sprayed on the fences.

Ask: How do you think he felt? How would all the makers of the garden feel? Have you ever felt like that?

Read together Isaiah 5.1–7.

Here God seems to be both the dreamer and the vandal. The prophet describes God's hopes for the people of Israel, God's care for the people – and their lack of response. Today we might say that God's creativity and dreams are met by human apathy and barrenness of imagination.

Discuss ways in which we can be seen as:
● the unproductive vineyard in Isaiah;
● the vandals in the modern story.

Yet the dream persists

Either let each member of a small group, or small groups within a larger one (or on your own) look at one or more of these readings: Genesis 1.1–5, 20–31; Isaiah 11.1–9; Isaiah 25.6–8; Isaiah 35.1–10; Isaiah 33.13–24.

Ask: What does this passage tell you about God's dreams for the world?

Share your reflections with the whole group.

Or listen while one person reads aloud the story of the hired labourers: Matthew 20.1–16.

Discuss how God responds to a broken and divided world with different values: grace, hope for all. How was this demonstrated in the coming of Christ?

PRAYER

Creative God,
Help us to understand and share
your dreams for the world.
Help us to work with them
and to be transformed by your grace
so freely given. Amen

... transformed
by your
grace ...

ACTION

● Look at the possibility of a garden project like the one described, in your neighbourhood. With whom would you share the dream?

● Write down steps to strengthen hope for yourself and those around you.

91

Study 4 *Transformation*

Keynote readings
Isaiah 61
Isaiah 43.16–21
Ezekiel 47.1–12
Revelation 22.1–2

AIM

To take a reflective rather than discursive approach to several Biblical passages about transformation, and thus open ourselves to be changed.

PREPARATION

You will need paper and paints or crayons (see below), space to spread the paper out on hard surfaces, and a source of music.

Read Isaiah 61.

Reflect on it. This could be done by listening to a quiet piece of music – classical, jazz or folk, but preferably just instrumental, no words – and at the same time making gentle patterns in paint (water-colour or ready-mixed children's paint) or chalk or crayon (pastel, water-soluble or wax), following the rhythms of the music. Coloured pencils or felt-tips can be used but are not so effective for this exercise. The idea is not to produce great art, but to let the words and their meaning enter into us in another way. If someone else reads the chapter aloud and you listen, the value will be even greater. It could be read through slowly twice, followed by a silence.

Discuss

What words or phrases spoke to you most strongly (e.g. verse 3, 'a garland instead of ashes'; verse 10, 'garments of salvation')?

Now **read Isaiah 43.16–21.**

Look at its imagery. How many ways does the image of water appear?

Water is another element, mysterious and powerful. It gives life and takes it away

Water is another element, mysterious and powerful. It gives life and takes it away. It is an agent of transformation. When water appears in our dreams it is often a sign of our emotional life – powerful, enriching, sometimes frightening, not always easy to understand. Sometimes reasoned words fail, where the language of dreams and poetry can communicate.

There is a story about water in the Old Testament which reminds us of how vital water is to any community, how valued in a dry, hot land, and how essential it was for an often beleaguered city like Jerusalem to know its sources of water and to protect them (see also Clare Amos' comments on this passage in *Words for Today*).

Read Ezekiel 47.1–12.

What do you find striking about this account? Does it remind you of any other biblical passage?

Now **read Revelation 22.1–2**, without comment, followed by silence and a prayer:

God of transformation, refresh us with living water,
take us out of our depth, trusting in you;
nourish the roots we often forget –
our deepest feelings and our dreams –
so that we may grow like trees beside a river,
standing tall, and bearing fruit. Amen

ACTION

In your own time, and with materials of your choice, make another picture, illustrating the verses from Revelation.

Study 5 *Do Dreams Come True?*

AIM

To grapple with the assumption that dreams are about unreality and visions about the unachievable.

Keynote readings
Jeremiah 18.1–11
Matthew 11.1–6
Acts 2.1–18

Comment

This session would ideally be accompanied by a clay meditation and Jeremiah 18.1–11 (see *Words for Today* for 1 September) – but Bibles and clay probably don't mix!

Ask

● What are the news headlines today? Go round the group, getting folk to remember and outline news stories. Remind them of the popular saying, 'It must be true – it's in the papers.' Is that always the case?

● When folk are wanting to 'put down' idealism, Christian hope, values which are different, they will contrast these with 'the real world'. What do they mean? Is the world they are thinking about more real?

● What is 'real' to you – because you live in the midst of it, it touches you, you care about it? Go round the group

What is 'real' to you?

So, where do dreams come from?

again, encouraging them to talk about home, family, neighbours, work, local community.

So where do dreams come in? Are they about unreality? Or about possibilities? That is, about the redemption or fulfilment of the world that is real to each of us?

Read Matthew 11.1–6.

What might be the equivalent of these 'signs' in our own community?

In his indirect (or very direct) answer to John's question, Jesus talked about the 'real' world (of poverty, suffering, prejudice) being completely changed. In his book *No Future without Forgiveness* (Rider, ISBN 07126–7013–0), Archbishop Desmond Tutu describes the work of the Truth and Reconciliation Commission in South Africa.

Its purpose was to enable the people of the new South Africa to move on from their terrible and divisive past, by granting amnesty for crimes committed by all sides during the apartheid struggle – but only if the perpetrators made a full public confession and disclosure of what they had done. They could not then be punished, nor could victims, or victims' families, bring any further action against them, although the state was prepared to offer compensation. The dream was of reparation, not retribution – but to achieve this, people had to face the ugly reality of what they had done – and suffered.

Many questioned whether such a visionary move, based on such a different set of values, could possibly succeed. But it did. If people asked, 'Where is the new South Africa?' the answer could be, 'The mourners are at last able to bury their dead … the guilty are set free from the burden of secrecy … the wronged have their names cleared … the victims have found it in their hearts to forgive … enemies are reconciled.'

In this case the dream did come true.

Read Acts 2.1–18, followed by a time of free prayer.

During the coming week use this prayer:

God of dreams and visions,
enable us to dream creatively and to listen to the
dreaming of others –

young and old – in our community.
May we be open to their ideas and see the reality of
their visions
and be encouraged, together, to hope. Amen

ACTION

Read the local papers, parish magazine, reports of Council meetings and Community Association minutes, and talk to your neighbours. What are the visions and dreams for your community? Are they unachievable?

Study 6 *God Beyond the Dreams*

AIM

To consider the way visionary moments relate to the rest of our lives.

Keynote readings
1 Kings 3.1–15
Acts 26.4–23
1 Timothy 1.15–17

Way in

Begin by emptying your pockets (or handbag) – or by gathering and placing on a table in front of you some of those small everyday objects which you take for granted, need frequently – and would feel lost without. If you are meeting in a group, you can enjoy a light-hearted comparison of what each has in front of them. If on your own, reflect: What do these things say about my responsibilities and my priorities?

Read 1 Kings 3.1–15.

Discuss

As Solomon prepared to take up a new responsibility – of becoming king after the death of his father David – what did he see as his priority? What might he have desired, in his dream? For what gift did he, in fact, ask God?

Solomon's dream was a preparation for the rest of his life. In dreams and visions, at moments in our lives which concentrate intense experience, we see things more clearly. But what follows?

On the island of Iona, off the west coast of Scotland, there is a weekly pilgrimage. For many years, folk who work for the Iona Community in the ancient Abbey and modern MacLeod Centre have led a group of their guests and day

Solomon's dream was a preparation for the rest of his life.

We cannot stay on the mountain-top. For each of us there is a whole world out there...

visitors around the island, pausing at points (at a stone cross, on the common grazing land, at the sea's edge) to reflect on our lives' journey. The pilgrimage has traditionally reached a 'high point' on the island's highest hill, Dun I. It is only 300 feet high, but from it the views on a clear day are breathtaking – distant islands and mountains, and the daily life of the island going on below. It is a reminder of those 'mountain-top experiences', those moments of clear-seeing and long vision, which are so important for our Christian journey. But we cannot stay on the mountain-top (as the disciples learned on the Mount of Transfiguration). For each of us there is a whole world out there, and having looked out over it, we need to travel on and become part of it, which will mean leaving behind the beautiful and visionary place.

Paul had a sudden vision on the road to Damascus, in which he saw things in a different light, and heard God speaking to him. He then had to find a way of being 'obedient to the vision'.

Read Acts 26.4–23.

Discuss
- Do you believe that everyone needs to have some special moment of spiritual vision if they are to come to a full commitment of themselves to Christ? If not, what else can draw people into such discipleship?
- What (or where) have been your 'mountain-top' or visionary moments?

How do these translate into the choices and responsibilities of daily life?

Look again at the things you put in front of you at the beginning.

PRAYER

Read 1 Timothy 1.15–17, and use it as your prayer.

ACTION

Reflect on what you may have learned in discussion about other people's visions and the way they work them out in daily life, and try to find ways of supporting and encouraging them. Remember that you can be encouraged and supported in the same way.

Find out more about the Iona Community by writing for information to:

The Warden/Deputy Warden
Isle of Iona
Argyll
PA76 6SN

NOTES BY
TINA BEATTIE

CHALLENGES FOR CHANGE

Study 1 *Why Change?*

Keynote readings
Isaiah 9.8–17
Jeremiah 23.1–4
Luke 16.14–18
Isaiah 1.11–20

*'Pursue justice,
guide the
oppressed...'*
Isaiah 1.16, REB

AIM

To identify fears and visions which we associate with change in ourselves, in our churches and in our societies.

PREPARATION

Have ready some quiet music, a large lump of modelling clay and a surface for people to work on.

Recognizing complacency

Martin Luther King was imprisoned in April 1963 for leading a civil rights demonstration without a permit. Eight Alabama clergymen issued a statement that called his activities 'unwise and untimely'. The following is an extract from Luther King's 'Letter from Birmingham Jail', in which he responds to his Christian critics:

'... Whenever the early Christians entered a town, the people in power became disturbed and immediately sought to convict the Christians for being 'disturbers of the peace' and 'outside agitators'. But the Christians pressed on, in the conviction that they were 'a colony of heaven', called to obey God rather than man. Small in number, they were big in commitment...

'Things are different now ... Far from being disturbed by the presence of the Church, the power structure of the average community is consoled by the Church's silent – and often even vocal – sanction of things as they are...

'If today's Church does not recapture the sacrificial spirit of the Early Church, it will lose its authenticity, forfeit the loyalty of millions, and be dismissed as an irrelevant social club with no meaning for the twentieth century...'

(Martin Luther King, 'Letter from Birmingham Jail', from A Peace Reader – Essential Readings on War, Justice, Non-

Violence and World Order, *edited by Joseph Fahey and Richard Armstrong, New York/Mahwah: Paulist Press, 1987)*

Read together Isaiah 1.11–20.

Then have a short time of silence while the group thinks together about their own lives and the Christian community to which they belong.

Talk together for a few minutes:
- Are you a disturber of the peace?
- Is your church regarded as a threat to the status quo?
- Do you feel threatened or anxious about being asked these questions?
- Why?

Role play
Act out a conversation with Martin Luther King; divide into pairs – one of you playing the role of a complacent white church-goer and the other playing the role of Luther King.

Afterwards reflect as a group on how you felt during this conversation.

Reflection
Gather around a table and take a piece of clay. With quiet music playing in the background, mould the clay into a shape. As you do so, imagine that you are the clay in the hands of God. How do you feel? How do you experience God's hands? Are they gentle, cruel, creative, bullying? Think about what you are doing with your hands. Does this help you to identify how you feel about opening yourself to changes that God might want to make in your life? Do you trust God to be creative and gentle? Do you fear that God will be destructive and cruel? Can you make a shape out of the clay that expresses something of your inner world in response to these questions? Keep that shape to reflect upon in the weeks that follow.

PRAYER

God, you mould the clay of all creation.
Your wonder is revealed to us in wind and rain, in sun and stars,
in all the beauty of our world.

Are you a disturber of the peace?

Yet we are afraid of being moulded by you
into the image of Christ.
Strengthen us, embolden us, and give us your grace,
so that we might pray with all our hearts,
'Let it be done to me according to your will.'

ACTION

Keep a note of the times you feel challenged in the week ahead. Think about how you respond, and about ways in which you might begin to see these difficulties as invitations to change. At the end of the week, identify one way in which you have begun to be changed, however small or insignificant that beginning might seem.

Study 2 *Hear the Cries of the Poor*

Keynote readings

Exodus 3.1–10
Amos 8.4–7
Luke 16.19–31
James 5.1–6
Hebrews 5.1–10
Isaiah 65.17–25

AIM

To explore images of God's kingdom in terms of justice, poverty and wealth.

Making connections
Read Amos 8.4–7.

Allow time to reflect on the reading in silence, and then repeat aloud any phrases or words which make an impression on you. Try to find out the meaning of any words which you do not understand.

● What does this reading tell you about the nature of God's judgement?

● In what ways do you think this reading applies to our world today?

● Identify some examples of ways in which the rich trample on the needy.

Rich against poor
Do this poverty quiz (taken from the *New Internationalist*, March 1999) and then look at the answers. Do any of the answers surprise you? Which ones?

1. In which country does one in nine people live in poverty?
   (a) South Africa; **(b)** Australia; **(c)** India; **(d)** Brazil.

'Here I am'

Exodus 3.4, REB

2. How much do the rich countries give to the much poorer ones every year?
   (a) Nothing; **(b)** $210 million; **(c)** $3,000 million; **(d)** $340,000 million.

3. 'Whenever you are in doubt or when the self becomes too much ... apply the following test: recall the face of the poorest and weakest man *(sic)* you have seen and ask yourself if the step you contemplate is going to be of any use to him. Will he gain anything by it? Will it restore him to a control over his own life and destiny? Then you will find your doubts and your self melting away.' Who said that?
   (a) Mahatma Gandhi; **(b)** Julius Nyerere;
   (c) Nelson Mandela; **(d)** President Suharto.

4. The world's 225 richest people have a combined wealth of over a million million dollars. This is the same as the annual income of how many of the world's poorest people?
   (a) 1 million; **(b)** 30 million;
   (c) 1 000 million; **(d)** 2 500 million.

5. In which country do 35.5 million people – one child in   four – live below the official poverty line?
   (a) Zambia; **(b)** Cambodia;
   (c) Russia; **(d)** United States.

6. 'I'm married and have a two-and-a-half-year-old daughter. I get up at 8.00 a.m.and don't have anything to eat until 7.00 or 8.00 p.m. I want my daughter to be able to eat.' Where is this person from?
   (a) Uganda; **(b)** Britain;
   (c) Aotearoa / New Zealand; **(d)** India.

7. Where do hundreds of thousands of rural people have no guaranteed water supply?
   (a) Pakistan; **(b)** Papua New Guinea;
   (c) Peru; **(d)** Australia.

8. What percentage of the UK population experienced a spell of poverty between 1990 and 1994?
   (a) 2%; **(b)** 53%; **(c)** 31%; **(d)** 7%.

'My people will build houses and live in them, plant vineyards and eat their fruit ... They will not toil to no purpose or raise children for misfortune.'
Isaiah 65.22–23, REB

*'Listen to this,
you that grind
the poor and
suppress the
humble...'*

Amos 8.4, REB

9. 'A substantial increase in the resources for fighting poverty in the poorest countries appears entirely affordable. It is a matter of political commitment.' Who said this?
(a) the World Bank; (b) the *New Internationalist*;
(c) the Canadian Government;
(d) Mozambique's Prime Minister.

10. The West gave the Third World $47.58 billion in aid in 1997. By what percentage was this different from the previous year?
(a) +2.5%; (b) +10%; (c) –7.1%; (d) –15.7%.

11. Who said, 'The new century is not going to be new at all if we offer only charity, that palliative to satisfy the conscience and keep the same old system of haves and have-nots quietly contained'?
(a) Nadine Gordimer; (b) Noam Chomsky;
(c) Boris Yeltsin; (d) Tony Blair.

12. In what part of the world has poverty increased seven-fold since 1988, pushing an additional 105 million people below the poverty line?
(a) Sub-Saharan Africa; (b) South America;
(c) The Pacific; (d) Former Soviet Union.

Answers

1 *(b)*

2 *(a) – the poor world gives to the rich in loan and debt repayments. Between 1983 and 1989, creditors in the rich world received $242 billion more from poor countries than they provided in new loans.*

3 *(a)*

4 *(d) – 47 per cent of the world's people.*

5 *(d)*

6 *(b)*

7 *All of them, including Australia.*

8 *(c)*

9 *(a) – in the 1990 World Development Report on poverty.*

10 *(c)*

11 *(a) – winner of the 1991 Nobel prize for literature.*

12 *(d)*

Now **read Amos 8.4–7** again, bearing in mind the picture of the world which the quiz reveals. How does this affect your reading of Amos?

PRAYER

May it come soon
to the hungry
to the weeping
to those who thirst for your justice,
to those who have waited centuries
for a truly human life.
Grant us the patience
to smooth the way
on which your Kingdom comes to us.
Grant us hope,
that we may not weary
in proclaiming and working for it,
despite so many conflicts,
threats and shortcomings.
Grant us a clear vision
that in this hour of our history
we may see the horizon
and know the way
on which your Kingdom comes to us.

*Grant us
patience...
Grant us
hope...*

(From Nicaragua, taken from Bread of Tomorrow,
edited by Janet Morley, SPCK/Christian Aid, London, 1995,
originally published in Windows into Worship,
edited by Ron Ingamells, YMCA, 1989).

ACTION

Consider subscribing to a magazine such as the *New Internationalist*, which will help you to become better informed about global issues of poverty. Find out about groups which campaign for a better deal on behalf of the world's poor, and think about ways in which you might support one of these. Buy Fair Trade products whenever possible, and boycott companies which violate ethical codes of practice.

New Internationalist
Tower House, Lathkill Street
Market Harborough LE16 9EF
Telephone 01858 439616

Study 3 *Change is Possible*

Keynote readings
Lamentations 3.19–26
Luke 18.18–30
Luke 19.1–10
Luke 19.45–48
Luke 20.1–8

AIM

To address feelings of frustration and impotence, and to come to a new sense of faith and hope in God's power to achieve change in and through us.

Preparation

Have ready some paper and pens.

Frustration and powerlessness

● Think of the last week's news. Identify one story which makes you feel helpless or disempowered.

● Focus on your feelings and try to put a name to them. Spend some time trying to understand why you feel as you do.

● What might help you to feel differently?

● Is this a situation you are able to change, in however small a way?

● If so, what might you do to contribute towards change?

Are you eager to take action?

● Reflect upon this question, and give a name to your feelings. Do you feel a sense of empowerment and hope? Are you eager to take action? Or do you feel threatened and burdened by having to take responsibility?

● Perhaps you conclude that this is a situation you cannot change. Think about how that feels. Do you feel acceptance, despair, defiance, rebellion, relief?

Change is possible

● Two decades ago fewer than half the people of the developing world had access to safe, clean water. Now more than two thirds have this most fundamental resource.*

● In the past 50 years poverty has fallen more than in the previous 500. Since 1960 child-death rates have halved and malnutrition has declined by a third. Developing countries have covered as much distance in human development during the past 30 years as the industrial world managed in over 100.**

* From The A to Z of World Development, *compiled by Andy Crump, edited by Wayne Ellwood (New Internationalist Publications, Oxford, 1998*
** *From the New Internationalist, March 1999*

After a few minutes' silence thinking about these facts, read together:

Sometimes

Sometimes things don't go, after all,
from bad to worse. Some years, muscadel
faces down frost; green thrives; the crops don't fail,
sometimes a man aims high, and all goes well.

A people sometimes will step back from war;
elect an honest man; decide they care
enough that they can't leave some stranger poor.
Some men become what they were born for.

Sometimes our best efforts do not go
amiss; sometimes we do as we meant to.
The sun will sometimes melt a field of sorrow
that seemed hard frozen: may it happen for you.

(*Sheenagh Pugh, from* Selected Poems, *Seren, 1990*)

PRAYER

Read Lamentations 3.19–26, slowly and prayerfully.

Allow the words to penetrate deeply so that they come into contact with some of your own feelings of despondency and hope.

Now write in your own words a short prayer or reflection which expresses some of these feelings.

> *Sometimes*
> *things don't go,*
> *after all, from*
> *bad to worse*

Study 4 *Pray for Change*

AIM

To consider the relationship between contemplation and action in the quest for peace.

A world at war

● Annual military spending in developing countries is $125 billion. Just 4% of this could achieve universal primary education, halve adult illiteracy and educate women to the level of men. Just 12% could provide health care and safe drinking water for all.

● Developed nations spend 30 times more on arms than on overseas aid.

Keynote readings
Daniel 6.10–22
Luke 11.5–13
Luke 18.9–14
1 Kings 8.22–23,
33–40
1 Timothy 2.1–8

- The permanent members of the UN Security Council supply most weapons to developing countries.
- About a quarter of the entire global scientific research and development budget is spent on defence and armaments and around half a million scientists are working on the development of new weapons.
- Torture occurs in more than 100 countries and is carried out as part of government policy in at least 40.
- Between 1990 and 1994, Britain supplied 13 per cent of total arms exports to sub-Saharan Africa.
- Over a million people have died in Iraq since 1990 as a direct result of sanctions.
- 2 000 people are involved in landmine accidents every month – one victim every 20 minutes. Around 800 of these will die, the rest will be maimed.

(Figures taken from The A to Z of World Development, *compiled by Andy Crump, edited by Wayne Ellwood, New Internationalist Publications, Oxford, 1998; and from issues of the* New Internationalist.*)*

Keep a few minutes' silence to think about these facts.

Read Luke 11.5–13.

- What are we really asking for when we pray for change?

Ask one member of the group to read this piece by Thomas Merton about praying for peace:

If people really wanted peace they would sincerely ask God for it and He would give it to them. But why should He give the world a peace which it does not really desire? The peace the world pretends to desire is really no peace at all.

To some people peace merely means the liberty to exploit other people without fear of retaliation or interference. To others peace means the freedom to rob others without interruption. To still others it means the leisure to devour the goods of the earth without being compelled to interrupt their pleasures to feed those whom their greed is starving. And to practically everybody peace simply means the absence of any physical violence that might cast a shadow over lives

'The peace the world pretends to desire is really no peace at all' (Thomas Merton)

devoted to the satisfaction of their animal appetites for comfort and pleasure.

Many people like these have asked God for what they thought was 'peace' and wondered why their prayer was not answered. They could not understand that it actually was answered. God left them with what they desired, for their idea of peace was only another form of war. The 'cold war' is simply the normal consequence of our corrupt idea of a peace based on a policy of 'every man for himself' in ethics, economics and political life. It is absurd to hope for a solid peace based on fictions and illusions!

So instead of loving what you think is peace, love other people and love God above all. And instead of hating the people you think are war-makers, hate the appetites and the disorder in your own soul, which are the causes of war. If you love peace, then hate injustice, hate tyranny, hate greed – but hate these things in yourself, not in another.

(Thomas Merton, from Seeds of Contemplation, *Anthony Clarke, 1972)*

● What are your reactions to this?
● Compare feelings about praying for peace with the facts of 'A world at war'.

If you love peace, then hate injustice, hate tyranny, hate greed ... in yourself

PRAYER

Let there be peace on earth, and let it begin with me.

Spend the last five minutes in silent waiting before God, offering to God one situation in which you experience anger, resentment or hostility towards an individual or a group. Try not to think or fret about this situation, but simply allow it to be part of your silence and part of your offering. See this as your soul's searching for the unfathomable mystery of God who is beyond all language, all knowing, all understanding. Expect nothing from the experience. It is enough simply to be unknowing and powerless before God. Try to spend five minutes like this each day during the week. At the end of the week, thank God for these times of silent contemplation.

ACTION FOR PEACE

Join a letter-writing campaign such as writing to a prisoner of conscience, or writing to your MP about the arms trade. For further information contact:

Amnesty International (British Section)
99–119 Rosebery Avenue
London EC1R 4RE

Campaign Against the Arms Trade
11 Goodwin Street
Finsbury Park
London N4 3HQ

Preparation for next week
Collect news cuttings about refugees in Britain.

Study 5 *A New Respect*

Keynote readings
Jeremiah 29.1, 4–7
Ruth 1.15–22
Ruth 3.1–18
Ruth 4.13–22

'Where you go,
I shall go'
Ruth 1.16, REB

AIM

To explore ways of welcoming the stranger and the outsider who invite us to leave behind old prejudices, and to open ourselves to new ways of being and relating.

PREPARATION

Have ready a small bowl of lavender oil and some quiet music.

Identifying the issues

● Read together the *Keynote readings* for this week and consider what they tell us about God's concern for refugees, strangers and oppressed groups.

● Discuss the newspaper cuttings you have collected. What do they reveal about attitudes towards refugees in Britain?

● Consider the terms 'asylum seeker' and 'illegal immigrant.' What do these words suggest to you? How do you think the language we use affects our attitudes towards others? Can you think of other examples?

● How might Christians challenge intolerance and hostility in British society?

Learning to look anew

A recent study conducted for the Home Office, called *The Settlement of Refugees in Britain*, notes that:

> The majority of asylum-seekers come with substantial work and educational qualifications, the bulk of which are under-utilized, to their chagrin and the country's general loss...

> There was a high rate of physical and psychological stress, largely consequent upon their past experiences that led individuals to seek asylum, and because of separation from their families. Virtually no help is being provided to help them cope with these difficulties.

Britain is sometimes described as a pluralist society, meaning that the country is home to many different ethnic and religious groups.

Read together:

A refugee's experience

Sou Huoy Lam left her home in Cambodia in the 1980s to seek asylum after her parents were killed when she felt herself to be endangered too. By this time the Pol Pot regime had ended, and the refugee camps in Thailand had been closed to newcomers, and Huoy had to sneak into a camp when the guards were not looking. To reach the camp she had to work her way through minefields.

Huoy's brother, who escaped three years earlier, was fortunate enough to be resettled in the United States. However, she and some others from the camp managed to get passports and a flight to Europe. But no country was prepared to admit them, and they found themselves 'in orbit' for 50 hours, being flown from one country to another.

Finally they were returned to Singapore, where it seemed they would be removed back to Thailand where they expected to be put in prison. Huoy's companion, Huy Lim, became so desperate at the thought of this that he slashed his wrists.

'Where you stay, I shall stay'
Ruth 1.16, REB

When everyone else had refused to accept Huoy, she was admitted to Britain because the plane she was flying on was British.

That was 10 years ago, and Huoy had not seen her brother since 1980. One of their last surviving relatives now lives in China, and they are planning a meeting together there.

Meanwhile Huoy has completed a degree in computing, and is using her skills in a job helping other refugees.

(From Keeping Hope Alive: Who finds refuge in Britain?, *Jesuit Refugee Service, Andes Press Agency, 1996)*

● Do you feel that the contribution Huoy makes to life in Britain is a positive one?

● In what other ways do you think immigrants to Britain have had a positive effect on British culture and society?

Anointing

Your people shall be my people, and your God, my God

Gather in a circle around a table, with a bowl of lavender oil in the middle and music quietly playing. Dip your finger in the oil and anoint the forehead of the person next to you, saying what Ruth said to Naomi: 'Your people shall be my people, and your God my God.' Pray that God will reveal to you your own prejudices, heal your fears, and bring you into a new place of loving openness to others.

PRAYER

Lord, make me an instrument of your peace;
Where there is hatred, let me sow love;
Where there is injury, pardon;
Where there is doubt, faith;
Where there is despair, hope;
Where there is darkness, light;
Where there is sadness, joy.

O Divine Master,
grant that I may not so much seek
to be consoled, as to console;
to be understood, as to understand;
to be loved, as to love;

for it is in giving that we receive,
it is in pardoning that we are pardoned,
it is in dying (to self) that we are born
to eternal life.
(Adapted from the Prayer of Saint Francis)

Where you die,
I shall die...'
Ruth 1.17, REB

ACTION

Be an instrument of peace. Contact the Refugee Council to find out how you can help ensure that asylum seekers are welcomed and their experiences and current situation properly understood:

The Refugee Council
3 Bondway
London SW8 1SJ

LOOKING AT LETTERS

Study 1 *From Contemporary Communications to Early Christian Correspondence*

Keynote readings

1 Thessalonians 1.1–3;
5.23–28
2 Thessalonians 1.1–4;
3.16–18
1 Corinthians 1.1–19
2 Corinthians
13.11–13

*'This greeting
is in my own
handwriting...'*
2 Thessalonians
3.17, REB

AIM

To study the form, content and value of different types of communication.

PREPARATION

● Write letters to all group members inviting them to bring to the next meeting a letter or greetings card which they treasure and would be prepared to share.

● Collect examples of: business letter; fax; e-mail; holiday postcard; advertising circular; 'begging' letter; letter to a newspaper; letter to an 'agony' aunt.

● Photocopy the Keynote readings.

● Make copies of the closing prayer.

Resources

● A flipchart or a large sheet of paper;
● Felt-tipped pens;
● A small table.

Getting started

Ask the group to spend five minutes looking at the examples of contemporary correspondence. List any other kinds of communication or correspondence they have received or sent. Ask members in pairs to share their reactions to all the correspondence displayed or noted. What do they tell us about the ways in which people communicate today? What problems or needs do they underline? Have members ever sent or received any of these forms of communication? If so, why did they choose to communicate in this way and what kind of response did they hope for? If not, why not? What are their most favoured and least liked forms of communication? Why?

Moving on

In plenary discussion, note which responses are common to all or a majority of the group, and those where there is divergence.

Going back

Ask for volunteers to read aloud the passages from Paul's letters listed above. Explain that these are examples of the form and content of the opening and closing sections of a typical early Christian letter. Note the key elements: identification of the sender and recipients, a specifically Christian greeting, a thanksgiving, and an ending which includes a wish for peace and some form of 'Grace'. Look at some or all of the following to see other examples of Paul's opening and closing greetings and the ways in which the standard form is occasionally altered or expanded:

● Galatians 1.1–2;
● Romans 1.1–7;
● Philippians 1.3–9; 4.21–23;
● Colossians 4.7–18.

For further study

James L Bailey and Lyle D Vander Broek, *Literary Forms in the New Testament*, SPCK, London, 1992, ISBN 0–281–04629–8, is a useful resource – particularly pages 23–31.

● Have members of the group ever received or sent letters with similar opening and closing greetings?

● In what circumstances might they write or receive such greetings?

● Why would such letters be valued?

● In what ways do they differ from some of the contemporary communications discussed earlier?

Treasured letters or cards

After a time of sharing, in whatever way seems appropriate, invite members to place their special letters or cards in the centre of the group and say the prayer together.

'Grace and peace to you...'
1 Corinthians
1.3, REB

We treasure the message of your love

Prayer

Loving God, we thank you for all the ways in which you keep in touch with us and communicate your living word.

Thank you for Saint Paul and all the letters he wrote to the churches he loved; for the time and trouble he took in the midst of his own difficulties, disappointments, hardships, imprisonment and pain to write words of encouragement, challenge and hope.

Thank you for those whose words have helped us. As we keep them close to our hearts may we treasure the message of your love and find new ways to pass it on.

Amen

Study 2 *Learning from Letters*

Keynote readings

1 Thessalonians
2.17–20; 3.7–9;
4.1–3, 7–12;
5.12–22
Philippians 1.3–8;
4.8–9
Ephesians 6.1–4,
10–18
Philemon 8–18

AIM

To apply the message of parts of St Paul's letters to those we might write today.

PREPARATION

● Make a large postcard and a greetings card with these messages in bold on one side:
Postcard: **Wish you were here**
Greetings Card: **Sorry we missed your birthday**

● Write these descriptions on small postcards (one per card):
  ○ A young person about to leave home for the first time to work or study.
  ○ An elderly church member who lives alone.
  ○ Parents of a baby recently baptized.
  ○ The members of a newly established church.
  ○ A newly converted Christian about to be released from prison.

● Photocopy the *Keynote readings* or have a list of the references for each member.

● Make copies of the prayer letter to God.

Resources

● Felt-tipped pens;

- Small sheets of paper;
- Pens or pencils;
- A small table.

Getting in touch
Ask members to recall moments in their lives or those of others known to them when they might have felt the need to say to God, 'I wish you were here.' Stress that these can relate to both joyful and sad occasions. Invite them to write brief details on the postcard. Do a similar exercise with the greetings card, asking members to recall the way in which they or others known to them celebrated Christmas, listing the ways in which the birthday of Jesus was forgotten or overlooked.

Staying in touch
In a short time of silence, invite members to think and pray quietly about what this says to them about the need to be in touch with God and the ways in which this contact can be broken.

Keeping in touch
Ask members in pairs to read the listed Bible passages. Give one of the postcards to each pair and ask them to think which of the passages might relate to the situation of the person or persons described, and to draft a letter in contemporary language to that person, using their own ideas and those expressed in any of the Bible passages which they consider relevant. Allow at least 30 minutes for this exercise and do not pressurize people to produce a 'polished' piece of prose. In plenary discussion, invite members to share what they have written and their thoughts and feelings about doing the exercise.

The local church keeping in touch
Ask members to suggest ways in which this exercise might be shared in their church to stimulate discussion and action about keeping in touch with the needs of others and helping one another to keep in touch with God. List all their ideas. Place the list and their draft letters on the table in the centre of the group.

Wish you were here

A prayer letter to God

Invite members in turn to sign this and ask if they would like to receive a copy to use as a further stimulus to prayer and action.

Dear God,

We are sorry that we have not kept in touch with you on a more regular basis. We will try to do better from now on. Thank you for not giving up on us and for all the messages of hope, encouragement, challenge and support we have received from you as we have studied and prayed together in this group. We promise that we will keep on trying to hear, apply and share them in our own lives and with others as we stay in closer touch with them and with you. This letter comes with our love and our prayers that you will help us to keep this promise and all our good intentions. Amen

Read it aloud on behalf of the group to close the meeting.

ACTION

Invite members to write letters or articles for the church magazine or newsletter to highlight some of the ideas and exercises they have shared, or to suggest ways in which the whole church might be more in touch with some of the needs they have explored.

NOTES BY
GRAEME BROWN

DAVID, THE POET KING

Study 1 *Music which Heals*

AIM

To think about how music can renew our health and to reflect on a song of the poet king which helped to restore his spirit.

Keynote readings
1 Samuel 16.1–23
1 Samuel 18.6–16
1 Samuel 19.1–18
2 Samuel 1.17–27

Your kind of music

● Let each member bring a cassette or CD of music or song which calms their minds and restores their spirits.

● Let each in turn play a part of their piece and explain why it affects them as it does. Is it the words or the music or both which calms them?

● Let members of the group respond to the choices of others.

The poet king

Music, poetry and dance, in contrast to fine art, all had a significant place in the culture of the Hebrew people, yet in few passages of the Bible is there any recognition of the link between music and the healing of the spirit. David, we are told, had many of the qualities which in those days made for a leader. He enjoyed the favour of God; he was 'a brave man and a fighter, prudent in speech, a man of presence'; and yet what in the first instance commended him to the court was his skill as a harpist.

High in the order of David's choice of the exploits by which he hoped to be remembered is his skill as 'the singer of the songs of Israel'. There seems little doubt that he calmed the spirit of King Saul with songs of his own composition. David was very soon recognised as a pop singer of his day.

The people's remedy
Read 1 Samuel 16.14–23; 18.6–9.

Can music restore health and renew the human spirit?

117

Saul's problem was paranoia, which was further stirred by the people's songs. It was, however, also from among the ordinary people who surrounded Saul, his servants and soldiers, that a remedy for his ailment was offered to the king. What they suggested seemed so readily acceptable to Saul that he sent for David without delay. There appears to have been almost universal acceptance in the court that music could have a role in therapy.

Listen again to 'the singer of the songs of Israel'

There has been widespread acknowledgement that some forms of sacred music are therapeutic. The popularity of Gregorian chants of monks of the Abbey of Santo Domingo de Silos in Spain has alerted many in the Church worldwide to the integrative effect of music upon the whole being. In Germany J S Bach's music draws crowds into packed churches at Christmas and Easter.

● Does it matter for the healing of our spirits whether the music is sacred music?

● Do any members engage in music therapy? Let them share their experience of this.

The people's choice
A survey in the United Kingdom has revealed that J G Whittier's hymn 'Dear Lord and Father of mankind' (often sung to Hubert Parry's tune *Repton*) is people's favourite hymn today.

● Read this hymn through quietly and prayerfully and consider why it is such a favourite. In what way does it speak to the condition of people today?

A song for the comfort of David
Read again David's own lament for Saul and Jonathan – 2 Samuel 1.17–27.

Spend a little time in silence and then share with the group your thoughts about how the composition of this poem and, perhaps, any accompanying music helped David to come to terms with this loss and to find a new serenity of spirit.

PRAYER

God, thank you for the music which makes us better.
Attune us to yourself that we may live in tune. We sing

*a new song and we share a new world and we dance to
the rhythm of a fresh new day. Amen*

ACTION

Choose a piece of music which you feel speaks to your
own spirit. Spend some time listening to it, allowing it,
perhaps, to bring its own gift of harmony to you. Give
thanks for the composer of the work, the players, singers
and those who have recorded the music. Write your own
brief poem of gratitude to God for the gift of music.

Study 2 *David the King*

AIM

To discern in David the leadership qualities which
brought stability to the nation and offered what later
generations considered to be a model for government.

Keynote readings
2 *Samuel 2.1–11*
2 *Samuel 5.1–12*
2 *Samuel 6.1–23*
2 *Samuel 7.1–29*

Warm-up

Ask the group to share their impressions of David as a
king.

● What, according to the key passages, were his
strengths?

● What were his weaknesses?

● What was it that made his successors regard his reign as
a golden age?

Reconciling interests

The symbolic value of Zion was important. David had
been king in Hebron, a village of his own tribe. When he
became king of all Israel, he forsook Hebron for a neutral
place which belonged previously to native people, the
Jebusites. In doing so David made a move which bridged
divergent interests. Jerusalem could become a focus of
reconciliation for the Hebrew people.

● Name some divergent interests in national politics
today.

● Do you think they can be overcome by imaginative
forgoing of traditional bases of power?

*David made a
move which
bridged
divergent
interests*

Is prosperity necessarily a sign that it is God who is making a person or nation prosperous?

Opting for simplicity

David had a palace built for himself in Jerusalem. It was symbolic of a certain prosperity. David believed that the nation was prosperous because of the blessing of God.

'David realized that the LORD had established him as king of Israel and was making his kingdom prosperous...' (2 Samuel 5.12, GNB)

What better than to acknowledge the source of his prosperity by the building of a temple for the Lord? What better than cementing his prosperity by bringing the covenant ark into David's city? There would be a sign that God's presence prospers people!

David's mentor, Nathan, was at first receptive to the idea, but the plan was scotched by the direct intervention of God. God said to Nathan in a dream: 'Tell my servant David that I say to him, "You are not the one to build a temple for me to live in. From the time that I rescued the people of Israel from Egypt until now, I have never lived in a temple; I have travelled round living in a tent."' (2 Samuel 7.5–6, GNB)

Buildings symbolize the aspirations of a generation.

● What buildings express our aspirations?

● How do you assess grandeur and simplicity in a building? Are grand buildings necessarily grandiose? Do simple buildings necessarily have simplicity?

● How far should we measure godliness by the yardstick of prosperity or of simplicity?

Politics for the people

'David realized that the LORD ... was making his kingdom prosperous for the sake of his people.' (2 Samuel 5.12, GNB)

David was probably one of the first rulers anywhere to recognize that those who rule do so for the sake of their people and not for their own self-aggrandizement.

The story of David's kindness to a disabled man, Mephibosheth, the son of Jonathan, seems designed to illustrate what ruling for the sake of his people actually means, although it is also clear that David wanted to keep a close eye on any descendant of Saul.

Read again 2 Samuel 8.15 – 9.13.

Let the group consider David's treatment of Mephibosheth in comparison with today's practice in the care of disabled people. In what respects is it acceptable or defective?

Meditation

King of our hearts, Christ makes us kings;
Kingship with him his servants gain;
With Christ, the Servant-Lord of all,
Christ's world we serve to share Christ's reign.
(*James Quinn, from* Church Hymnary, *3rd Edition*)

ACTION

Consider, if you haven't done so already, joining a political party in solidarity with those who seek to influence the style of government in the country.

Study 3 *King David, Just Human, but also Just*

AIM

To reflect on how Nathan and David handled David's moral lapse and how failure may be managed constructively and life begin again.

Let's have it out in the open

The poet-prophet Nathan, with great courage, went to see David in private and told him a story.

Read 2 Samuel 12.1–15.

Take some minutes to consider:

● What feel do you get of the relationship that existed between these two men?

● Do you have an impression that Nathan had prepared carefully for this meeting?

● What are the literary qualities of Nathan's story which drew such an immediate and angry response from David?

● What does David's response say about David's own sense of justice?

The question to ask of government is this: 'For whom are you ruling?'

Keynote readings
2 Samuel 8.15
2 Samuel 11.1–27
2 Samuel 12.1–25
2 Samuel 23.1–5

How best can we accompany others through failure to restoration?

- What common basis in faith existed between David and Nathan?

- 'You are the man!' Nathan calls David's action 'evil disobedience to God.' This approach seems confrontational, but does it work?

- Does Nathan give more attention to the conspiracy to have Uriah killed or to David's act of adultery?

- David very simply admits his sin and receives God's forgiveness, but what is the effect of his sin upon his family?

Nathan ends the interview abruptly.

Adultery causes more heartache and family distress in contemporary society than perhaps any other breach of loyalty or act of injustice.

Take time to talk through the questions raised above.

- How does the group assess Nathan's skill in handling this situation?

- Are there any lessons to be learned in the managing of failure?

- Are we too cautious in naming and confronting evil? If this is so, why is it so?

- Is our own sense of injustice in relation to adultery and the betrayal of others blunted by the mores of contemporary society?

Justice in society

Court historians in Israel had an unenviable task. They knew about the complex nature of David's personal relationships. They did not seek to cover up his well-known acts of flagrant injustice. But they also knew that basically his heart was in the right place and tried to say so: 'David ruled over all Israel and made sure that his people were always treated fairly and justly.' (2 Samuel 8.15, GNB)

This assessment has about it the feel of the flattery of the court praise-singer, but also contains a significant element of truth.

The Sun King

David did begin again and turned his attention to ruling justly. He wrote poems in which he attempted to set out what he believed about his rule:

The protector of Israel said to me:
'The king who rules with justice,
    who rules in obedience to God,
is like the sun shining on a cloudless dawn,
    the sun that makes the grass sparkle after rain'
(2 Samuel 23.3–4, GNB)

There have been many examples in history of sun kings who were notoriously unjust and of fundamentalist regimes, based on principles of divine law, which were ruthless. It is tempting to give up the search for just government which is based on obedience to God and to settle for rule based on human rights without reference to God.

● Share in the group your vision of what government will be like which has the characteristic of 'the sun shining on a cloudless dawn'.

PRAYER

God, you rule the world with justice. Enshrine your presence at the heart of politics that your ways may be the model for our laws and your loving kindness the measure of our policies. So may the sun shine on a cloudless dawn, the grass sparkle and the whole earth be clothed with Christ, the King. Amen

ACTION

Is there a political issue of the day about which you feel strongly and on which you might write a letter of encouragement to someone engaged with the issue?

'...the sun shining on a cloudless dawn'
2 Samuel 23.3,
GNB

NOTES BY
ANNA BRIGGS

GOD WITH US

Study 1 *David's Descendant – What's in a Name?*

Keynote readings
Jeremiah 33.14–16
Matthew 1.17–25
Matthew 22.41–45
John 3.1–17
Colossians 1.15–20
Romans 15.4–13
Isaiah 2.1–5

And he named the child Jesus.
Matthew 1.25, REB

AIM

To look at what might disturb our tight hold on our 'sacred' things.

PREPARATION

Have on a table in the middle of the group some or all of the following:
● a map;
● a globe;
● a heraldic crest (a blazer with a school or team badge will do);
● two passports (an EU passport, an 'old' British one or one of those fake British black covers you can buy, and one of another nationality);
● a family Bible with family tree.

Prayer

Christ, who was, and is, and is to come, you are our way, you are our signpost, you are our destination, yours is the name we bear while we travel and when we arrive. Be with us through our Advent journey, and lead us to the stable to find you again, a helpless baby, bringing us gifts we have not yet dreamed of. We pray to you, God, who made us, with you, Spirit, who comforts us, in the name of Jesus, our Saviour. Amen

What's in a name – and why does it matter?

Have each member of the group in turn pick up one of the things on the table (you can use the same ones more than once) and tell the group something about where he or she comes from and what he or she knows about his or her family origins (two minutes each – be firm).
● Do common themes emerge?

Read Jeremiah 33.14–16.

● How important was it for Jesus' followers to show that he was connected to David – that those who called him 'Messiah' could point to the Hebrew prophets as authority? In 21st century Western culture, does any such authority remain?

● Who will promise us 'safety'? Listen to those responding to the latest budget. The only question asked is, 'What's in it for me?' The interviewer tries to trap the Chancellor by asking if he's trying that old socialist trick of redistributing wealth.

● What would 'justice and righteousness' look like today? Could we all agree, even on some basic principles?

● So what authority do our leaders have?

● Does any of us have a sense of history which will help us to answer these questions?

Read Matthew 22.41–45.

● Was Jesus brought up hearing again and again that he was a Son of David? He was certainly brought up to know the Scriptures, and was able to recall them appropriately throughout his life. But here he turns the scripture on its head, challenging the Pharisees in their ordered way of thinking. None of them was able to answer him, we are told. In his life Jesus turned many sacred things on their heads. He made friends with tax-collectors and prostitutes, made fishermen his followers, let the noisy children come to him.

● What 'sacred' things of today would he overturn?

● Can you imagine Jesus in the stock exchange, with the consultant on a ward round, at a university graduation ceremony, or even at our church meeting?

● Would we hold on so tightly to our sacred things if we knew Jesus?

Jesus turned many sacred things on their heads

Discussion time
You have time to discuss these issues almost to the end of your study group meeting.

Leave five minutes at the end to discuss possible action – e.g. find out what is being offered locally to refugees from recent wars in Europe and Africa. Could your church be more involved? Is there some way you could help refugees to feel more at home, to help them recover the past they have lost? What stories have they got to tell? Can you find ways to be the audience for that story-telling? Could the group write the intercession for Sunday worship, reflecting some of these questions?

Close with the Lord's Prayer and Grace.

Study 2 *The Coming Kingdom*

Keynote readings
Isaiah 52.1–12
1 Kings 18.17–39
Amos 5.4–15
Jeremiah 7.1–15
Ezekiel 34.1–16
Isaiah 40.1–11
Matthew 3.1–12

AIM

To ask what the new kingdom will be like, and what are our idols today.

PREPARATION

Have on a table in the middle of the group the following:
- A five- or ten-pound note;
- CDs from top rock groups;
- a credit card;
- a fashion item with a designer label or logo (e.g. a Gucci bag or make-up bag or a photo of one from a magazine, a Reebok trainer shoe);
- car keys;
- a football team shirt;
- a Rolex watch (or a picture of one);
- a Jubilee 2000 badge or chain;
- a floppy disk;
- a pack of cigarettes;
- a bottle of wine or a can of beer.

A helpless baby, bringing us gifts we have not yet dreamed of

Prayer

Christ, who was, and is, and is to come, you are our way, you are our signpost, you are our destination, yours is the name we bear while we travel and when we arrive. Be with us through our Advent journey, and lead us to the stable to find you again, a helpless baby, bringing us gifts we have not yet dreamed of. We pray to you, God, who made us, with you, Spirit, who comforts us, in the name of Jesus, our Saviour. Amen

What do we worship?

Have each member of the group pick up one or two of the items from the table and tell the others what she or he could not be without. Do common themes emerge?

Read 1 Kings 18.17–39.

The prophet Elijah patiently waits for the people to worship their gods. He even helps them to prepare the sacrifices, making sure that they spare no effort. So God today watches patiently while we offer our sacrifices to the all-too-well-known gods – run up our credit card accounts then worry about paying them, insist on the latest car or fashion item, put anything and everything before our integrity and faith.

Read Jeremiah 7.1–15.

Jeremiah shows less patience than Elijah did in the first reading – this passage, containing the words Jesus quoted when he cleansed the temple, shows that at different times in the history of Israel God's warnings are conveyed more or less strongly. But the words of mercy are clear – God wants nothing more than to live with people who have cleansed themselves of all that is wrong in the way they live.

Read Matthew 3.1–12.

The mercy promised by Jeremiah is realized in the baptism of repentance offered by John. Appealing to their ancestors was no way for people to deliver themselves from God's wrath – and John promises a greater baptism yet in the person of Jesus Christ.

● Think how the promise of the world is 'bigger and better', too – the machine or powder which cleans everything, the bank loan which will change your life, and so on.

● How are these promises different from the promise John makes?

Discuss the readings and questions raised until the last five minutes.

Discuss what action you could take.

The young people of the Ecumenical Church Centre in Livingston, Scotland, have painted a giant mural for their

'Clear a road through the wilderness...'
Isaiah 40.3, REB

roof – a huge trainer, the very latest, with its cost alongside, compared to an Asian worker sewing the trainer and the weekly wage he or she receives.

- Is there any way your church could act to reflect these modern icons to the world which worships them?
- Are you prepared for the hostility it might cause?
- Could you work with a local workforce to show up some of these values when their own labour is poorly rewarded and their livelihood threatened by change?
- Could the group write the intercessions for Sunday worship, reflecting some of these questions?

Close with the Lord's Prayer and Grace.

Study 3 *Living on the Edge (A Voice in the Wilderness)*

Keynote readings
Luke 1.57–66
Luke 1.67–79
John 1.19–28
Luke 3.10–14, 18–20
Matthew 11.7–15
Matthew 11.16–19
Luke 1.46–55

'What will this child become?'
Luke 1.66, REB

AIM

To find out where we come from, and where we are called to go.

PREPARATION

Have on the table in the middle of the group as many as possible of the following:
- a birth certificate;
- a book about a modern leader who has spent time in prison, e.g. Steve Biko, Nelson Mandela or Irina Ratushinskya;
- a TV soap weekly magazine.

Prayer

Christ, who was, and is, and is to come, you are our way, you are our signpost, you are our destination, yours is the name we bear while we travel and when we arrive. Be with us through our Advent journey, and lead us to the stable to find you again, a helpless baby, bringing us gifts we have not yet dreamed of. We pray to you, God, who made us, with you, Spirit, who comforts us, in the name of Jesus, our Saviour. Amen

- Are you named after anyone special?
- Do you have a sense of vocation?

Discuss these questions with each other:

- How have your name, family tradition and expectations ordained the course of your life?

- Have you done things differently, gone out on a limb?

Read Luke 1.57–66.

This is an unusual pregnancy. Elizabeth is past the age of childbearing, and apparently barren. Her husband is even older, so something different is happening here. Still, instead of following tradition, these faithful Jews are together in one thing, and Zechariah's silence is not broken until the child is named 'John'. The neighbours wonder what will become of the child.

- Where did Nelson Mandela, Irina Ratushinskya, and Steve Biko get their vocation from?

- Why did it light on them and not on the next person? For any of the three, their actions could have led to their death (and in Biko's case, it did).

Read Matthew 11.16–19.

When the old traditions are lost, the signs are hard to read. I watch the soaps and chat shows, and in both fact and fiction, people seem to be making it all up as they go along. The *Eastenders'* Mitchells claim to stick by 'family' but they don't do it very consistently. The chat shows are terrifying to watch. Can you imagine that people would willingly expose their feuds and their follies, and look for answers? People could find fault with John the Baptist for his austerity, and with Jesus for consorting with the 'wrong sort'. One twentieth century leader told us 'there is no such thing as society, only a collection of individuals'. So why do some people hold out, and others look for the easiest way?

Don't just talk about 'they' – we're all in this world

Silently **read the** *Magnificat* **(Luke 1.46–55) and the** *Benedictus* **(Luke 1.67–79).**

Discuss how things have changed.

- Does anyone have a sense of living in the faith tradition?

- How can the Church offer that faith tradition to the world of chat shows, soaps, and shopping malls? (Don't just talk about 'they'. We're all in this world too).

Five minutes before the end talk about what action the group or church can take to do this. Could you set up a display in your shopping mall, with an exhibition of your church activities and why you all belong? Can you find a way to invite people in, or take worship to them? (The chaplain at Gateshead Metro Centre leads worship there every week). Look at your hymn book. Are there any hymns which reflect this discussion? Could you write one together?

End with the Lord's Prayer and Grace.

Study 4 *Born of God*

Keynote readings
Luke 1.26–45
Luke 2.1–20
Titus 2.11–14
John 1.1–18
Revelation 5.1–14
Revelation 22.6–21
1 John 3.16–24
1 John 4.7–21

AIM

To find out more about what it means to be born of God.

PRAYER

Christ, who was, and is, and is to come, you are our way, you are our signpost, you are our destination, yours is the name we bear while we travel and when we arrive. Be with us through our Advent journey, and lead us to the stable to find you again, a helpless baby, bringing us gifts we have not yet dreamed of. We pray to you, God, who made us, with you, Spirit, who comforts us, in the name of Jesus, our Saviour. Amen

Read:

I am the great sun

I am the
great sun,
but you
do not
see me

I am the great sun, but you do not see me,
  I am your husband, but you turn away.
I am the captive, but you do not free me,
  I am the captain you will not obey.

I am the truth, but you will not believe me,
  I am the city where you will not stay,
I am your wife, your child, but you will leave me,
  I am that God to whom you will not pray.

I am your counsel, but you do not hear me,
  I am the lover whom you will betray,
I am the victor, but you do not cheer me,
  I am the holy dove whom you will slay.

I am your life, but if you will not name me,
   Seal up your soul with tears, and never blame me.

(Charles Causley, from The Sun Dancing,
edited by Charles Causley, Penguin Books Ltd, 1982)

Now read John 1.1–18.

Spend five minutes in silence, thinking about these readings.

Then, have each member write down one or two of the words which have stuck in his or her mind, and put them in a small bowl or basket in the centre of the group.

Read Isaiah 7.10–16, Luke 1.26–45 and Revelation 22.6–21.

When it came to describing the relationship between God and Emmanuel/Jesus, most of the writing was – and still is – poetic. From Isaiah and John the Gospeller, from John the writer of Revelation to Charles Causley and countless other poets and hymnwriters, only poetry would rise to the level needed to describe this central truth of faith.

● Are Jesus' parables in themselves really the poetic use of everyday experience? Our imagination is drawn to new possibilities for human existence.

● Did Luke mean us to take his account of Jesus' conception and birth any more literally than we take the Prologue of John's Gospel or the visions of Revelation?

Many acts of faith are poetic rather than literal. We use water in baptism, rings in marriage, and bread and wine in Communion, knowing that they stand for something much greater but just as real. But we live in a literal world, full of facts and statistics.

● How can we use the images of today to catch the imagination of people who live in this world?

ACTION

Use the discussion of these questions to write a prayer using powerful modern imagery (e.g. space travel, technology, ecology) yet still poetic. Find one of Brian Wren's best hymns, 'Bring many names', and (if you have a CopyCare licence at your church) ask for it to be used in

Many acts of faith are poetic rather than literal

worship and then use the response to it as a ground for further discussion.

Close with the basket of words you all wrote earlier and put in the middle, and offer your new prayer, the Lord's Prayer, and the Grace.

NOTES

OTHER IBRA PUBLICATIONS

DISCOVERING CHRIST SERIES

Explore a range of issues and questions with writers of widely different experiences and cultures. They challenge us to see beneath a comfortable approach to Christian festivals, to recognize Christ among the poor and those who suffer. Yet they are by no means 'kill-joys'. They also share with us something of the joy and fun of celebration in each context.

The series is edited by Maureen Edwards, and contributors include Barbara and David Calvert, Sheila Cassidy, Magali do Nascimento Cunha, Alec Gilmore, Melvyn Matthews, Israel Selvanayagam, Bernard Thorogood and Pauline Webb.

Books in this series include:
- *Advent and Christmas;*
- *Ascension and Pentecost;*
- *Lent and Easter.*

ONLINE TO GOD

Can prayer be fun?

Written by children and young people from many parts of the world, *Online to God* is an exciting book of new prayers for 7–12-year-olds. Laughter, jokes, feelings and everyday happenings are shared and talked over with God.

Enjoy the cartoons, activities and crosswords linked with the prayers. Some of these can be tried out on friends or family!

This is a book for children and young people, but also a valuable resource for group leaders, teachers, parents and others who want to encourage young people to explore prayer and discover that it *can* be fun.

Order through your IBRA Representative, or from the appropriate address on page 136.

Our partners overseas

The IBRA International Fund, available through the generous donations of many readers, helps Christian organizations in developing countries to produce their own Bible reading notes. Some are reproduced in English, but most are translated and printed locally. In many cases we supply the book covers and the film ready for printing. Sometimes we supply the text and a grant towards local production, thus helping to provide local employment as well as encouragement to read the Bible regularly.

Bible reading cards giving the daily texts are translated into several languages and distributed, usually without charge, to many parts of the world.

It is difficult to estimate the exact number of people reading the daily Bible passages throughout the world, but it may be in excess of half a million.

In Christian service

IBRA has been serving the World Church since 1882. Now, at the beginning of a new millennium, we look to the future with renewed vision and enthusiasm to provide the necessary means to enable the Church worldwide to meet some of its publishing and resources needs.

As the Christian world opens up, communities responding to the Christian message need books and resources to learn and understand. These are often too expensive in the developing world, which is why the International Fund of IBRA – A Really Bright Idea! – needs your help.

Help us to increase the number of people regularly reading the Bible through our Bible reading notes and cards, by:

- Giving generously – speak to your IBRA Representative or write to the appropriate address on page 136 for details of covenants, donations and legacies. The only money we have to use is the money you give.

- Praying for all who are involved in the work of IBRA, both in the UK and overseas.

INTERNATIONAL BIBLE READING ASSOCIATION

– a worldwide service of the National Christian Education Council
at work in five continents.

HEADQUARTERS

1020 Bristol Road
Selly Oak
Birmingham
Great Britain
B29 6LB
and the following agencies

http://www.ncec.org.uk
ibra@ncec.org.uk

AUSTRALIA

Uniting Education (previously The Joint Board of Christian Education)
PO Box 1245 (65 Oxford Street)
Collingwood
Victoria 3066

GHANA

IBRA Secretary
PO Box 919
Accra

INDIA

All India Sunday School Association
PO Box 2099
Secunderabad – 500 003
Andhra Pradesh

NEW ZEALAND

Epworth Bookshop
PO Box 6133, Te Aro
75 Taranaki Street
Wellington 6035

NIGERIA

IBRA Representative
PMB 5298
Ibadan

SOUTH AND CENTRAL AFRICA

IBRA Representative
Box 1176
Sedgefield 6573
South Africa